PENGUIN BOOKS

cyberscene

Okay, the **Net** is here and it's not about to go away. So you **need** this book – to make sure you **make the most** of the Net without going mad in the process.

Cyberscene is **IT**...

● Learn how to make your mark on the Net ● See a guy with a video camera attached to his head (not a good look . . .) ● Watch the first Internet Soapie ● Visit the Official Santa Virtual Community ● Improve your homework and your research skills (really) ● Make your own multiple personalities ● Chat with the experts – about almost anything ● Interact with thousands of aliens and have 1000% more fun!

By the time you reach the end, you'll be great at being cyber. You'll be so **wired** you'll even be able to make **your own mark** on the amazing cyber scene.

cyber
a teen tr

NICK MORAITIS

[penguin books]

scene

aveller's guide to the web

Penguin Books Australia Ltd
487 Maroondah Highway, PO Box 257
Ringwood, Victoria 3134, Australia
Penguin Books Ltd
Harmondsworth, Middlesex, England
Penguin Putnam Inc.
375 Hudson Street, New York, New York 10014, USA
Penguin Books Canada Limited
10 Alcorn Avenue, Toronto, Ontario, Canada M4V 3B2
Penguin Books (N.Z.) Ltd
Cnr Rosedale and Airborne Roads, Albany, Auckland, New Zealand
Penguin Books (South Africa) (Pty) Ltd
4 Pallinghurst Road, Parktown 2193, South Africa

First published by Penguin Books Australia Ltd, 1999

10 9 8 7 6 5 4 3 2 1

Designed and typeset by Ruth Grüner
Printed in Australia by Australian Print Group, Maryborough, Victoria

National Library of Australia
Cataloguing-in-Publication data:

Moraitis, Nick.
Cyberscene: a teen traveller's guide to the web.

Includes index.
ISBN 0 14 130209 7.

1. World Wide Web (Information retrieval system) – Juvenile literature.
2. World Wide Web (Information retrieval system).
3. Internet (Computer network) – Juvenile literature.
4. Internet (Computer network). I. Title.

004.67

www.penguin.com.au

Publisher's note:

It has not always been possible for us to trace the original sources for the material used in this book, as these sources were located on the Internet. However, our known sources are detailed in the acknowledgements on page 169.

The content of the websites listed in this book, due to the constantly changing face of the Internet, may change considerably from the content cited at the time of publication. Penguin Books therefore cannot be held responsible for the content, or the accessibility, of those sites listed.

acknowledgements

A huge big thank you to my publishers Penguin Books for not laughing too much when I said I wanted to write a book, especially my editors, Suzanne Wilson and Erica Irving, and my designer Ruth Grüner. Also thanks to Robyn Annear for helping me along the way.

Also, a huge big thank you to my mum, dad and Pam for providing me with millions of hours of Internet access (before I bankrupted them, and had to pay myself!), my grandma who kept trying to get me to go to bed before 11 o'clock (in vain!), my class 9R who gave me the original idea, my school mentor Mr Comerford, and Cheryl from the World Kids Network who taught me that, 'If you can dream it, you can do it!' Then there are my enthusiastic readers and friends, Steve, Sean, Paul, Sarah, Thea and Jeremy – thanks! Also to Tom and Kristel at TCN who somehow managed to explain to me (just before going to press), that I had all the complexities of Bits and Bytes very very wrong (I think I now qualify as a nerd?).

Thanks also to absolutely everyone I've ever met! (I've always thought someone should put that in: you never know how you've been influenced, inspired and helped by those around you . . .).

Nick Moraitis

CO

RealAudio

contents...

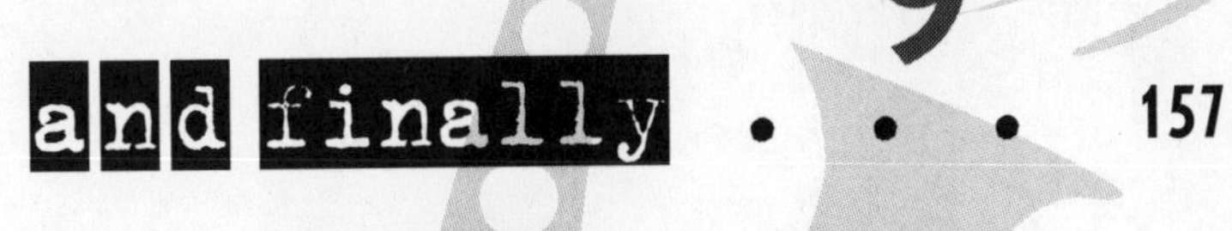

9 and finally . . . 157

newbies you better read this!

chapter zero
introduction

introduction

So you've heard about this thing called the Internet and maybe know a couple of things about it . . .

Some words like cybersurfing and superhighway ring a bell? You want to know more? Well, you have come to the right place! ¶

First things first. I'd like to introduce myself. My name is Nick and I'm a teenager from Melbourne, Australia. I've always been interested in computers and what computers could do, so when I heard some early hype about the Net, I couldn't wait to hook in and see what it was like.

When I first used the Internet 3 years ago, I knew almost nothing about it. I knew it was some kind of electronic information that I accessed using a computer, but apart from that – nothing!

For the first little while I had a lot of trouble doing anything, but after a few weeks of trial and error everything seemed to start to work when I wanted it to. As I'll explain later, there are some things which you can learn about the Internet, but often I've decided (quite unscientifically) that whether you can get things to work or not comes down to plain old luck.

For 2 years I've been busy designing and producing an on-line club for teenagers interested in computers called the Teenage Computer Network, or simply TCN. I've had lots of requests for help concerning all the sections of the Internet, from sending messages, to looking up information.

Often people ask me why the Internet would be useful for them – and my answer is always different. The Internet can do ***so*** many different things, for so many different people – from getting fan and contact information on your favourite actor, to making the most of computer games by playing them against other real people, or even finding information for your next school project.

This book is my attempt to help everyone else like me learn about these new technologies. It's ***not*** a technical user's manual to the Internet, and it's ***not*** a catalogue of Internet websites (which would become out-of-date very quickly), but a simple guide to becoming Net-savvy. By the time you reach the end, you should know what the Internet is, how to use it to help you, and finally, you should know something about adding your own mark to the 'on-line world'.

The first couple of chapters get you going on the Net and after you've got that out of the way, you can continue on your journey. The rest of the book is dedicated to showing you what you might find on-line. It's designed to give you some inspiration, so you can go away and discover what the Internet really has to offer.

I'm not going to assume that you know lots about the Internet already, just a very small bit about the basics (as long as you can type on a word processor you've got all the skills I need). I'll try to take it all right from the start.

However, because I don't find it incredibly interesting (and because I'm sure you wouldn't either), I've skipped a lot of the detail on the connecting and most technical information altogether. Let someone else do all that stuff, and you can concentrate on becoming a 'Net king' (or queen, as the case may be).

Being 'cyber' or 'wired' is actually a bit of a joke among the Net community. A little while ago it was 'uncool' to be a skinny computer nerd: the type of person who had huge square glasses and drank extra caffeine to keep him (always of the male gender) awake at night on the Net.

The fashions of Internet style, known to the long-time users (those connected for more than 6 months) are very different to what is generally thought of in the off-line world. A nerd is now a 'cool' thing to be. New Netters, who've just come on-line, seem always to get caught out by the hype and incorrect (or perhaps just out-of-date) articles on Net style they read in the newspapers. I'll tell you now that calling yourself a 'wired, surfing, cyberpunk' will only get you laughed at. 'Cyberpunk', which has always been a word used satirically by the Net community, is really 'uncool'.

So what ***is*** 'cool', you might say? Well, for one, never admitting that you are. Just go with the flow, act as if all that Netspeak, the jargon and the acronyms are your first language and you'll get along fine. If there's one thing Netters hate it's the new user or 'newbie' pretending they are the god of the system. As long as you are comfortable with the style and are a few more steps up in the 'hip' ladder than the rest of the non-Net population you'll be on your way to becoming a professional Net user. All this requires is some witty lines and a careful mouth.

And a word of advice. Treat everything you read on-line with scepticism and then later, check back to make sure it wasn't serious.

Nick Moraitis, 1999

P.S. **'Cool'** is the most 'uncool', out-of-date and overused word you can find on-line. That's why I've deliberately overused it in this introduction to prepare you for what's to come. Don't be **uncool** – **don't** use the word 'COOL'.

Nerd Liberation Movement ★ "Coming Out of the Basement"

hooking up
to the Net

chapter one

and how it all works

what can the Internet do?

- Give you instantaneous mail delivery
- Let you chat to a friend on the other side of the world
- Make you spend half your life reading about other people
- Let you listen to live concerts
- Give you on-line games – battle against other real people for supremacy
- Let you check the public library for books without leaving home
- Have you spend the other half of your life putting stuff about yourself on-line for other people to read!

The **Internet** can do **all this** and **much more!**

How? *I hear you ask!*

Ah well, that's the **tricky bit**. It can do all that because the Internet is what people call **a network**. That's just a name for a lot of computers **connected together** all **communicating** with each other.

In fact, the Internet is the largest network in the world. Computers store information inside them on things called disks. For example, when you write a story on a word processor you usually save it to the hard disk.

When you 'network' a bunch of computers (by linking them together in one way or another) you make the information on each computer available to everyone else extremely quickly.

Networks also let you send information to any other computer connected to the network. But unlike normal networks the Internet is not just *one* big computer with many other computers accessing its information. It's a lot of computers all accessing *each other's* information.

This may all seem very complicated but there is actually a very simple and handy reason behind it. The Internet was originally an American strategical military device invented way back in the 60s. At the time, people were just starting to put all the top secret information and weapon control systems onto computers, but they realised that they had a problem. If the opposition found out where these computers were stored then they could simply send in some scary secret agents to blow them up. In one easy stroke they would lose control of all those nuclear targeted missiles.

So they got a few more computers and put them far apart and then 'Internetted' them. Now they had lots of computers all with exactly the same information. If one was ever sabotaged, they always had plenty of backups, because they didn't need each other to work. And it's still the same now. If one computer connected to the Internet stops being connected, it doesn't normally affect the other computers connected.

wired words

Yes, I admit it – the Web is full of lots of really hard, meaningless words (until you know what they mean of course!). Before we get into the rest of the book, and so that you know some of the terms before you really get into things, here's a few of them.

BANDWIDTH

Bandwidth is what everyone who has ever been on the Internet wants more of. In fact, it's very much like (you guessed it!) a superhighway. Just as a superhighway with more lanes of traffic can carry more cars, a network such as the Internet, with more bandwidth, can carry more information or data. And just like a superhighway, if the bandwidth is bigger, the faster you can go! Bandwidth can be carried over cables or can even be beamed through the air. As I said before, if you have more cables, you have more bandwidth. At different places along the many routes of the highway, the road of cyberspace gets narrower, and then widens out. You can't control most of these sections (it's up to the companies that own them), but you can usually get more bandwidth coming directly to your house (a bit like a bigger, better driveway going into your garage) by paying extra for your Net connection.

BITS/BYTES

Bits and bytes are units just like metres or litres. But instead of measuring distance or volume, bits and bytes measure information stored in a computer. A bit is actually a '1' or a '0' and a byte is a collection of eight bits. Together, bits can represent things such as letters and numbers. This is where it gets confusing. A kilobit, or 'k' (which is commonly used on the Web when measuring speed) is one thousand bits, while a kilobyte is one thousand bytes. So a megabyte is one million bytes and a megabit is one million bits. And that is where I stop boring you to death, and as far as I can count on two hands . . .

BROWSER

If bandwidth is a superhighway, then a browser is a car, a software program that takes you from place to place. Usually browsers are used for the multimedia part of the Internet called the World Wide Web – but they can now be used for other aspects as well. A browser doesn't actually do anything except get the specific information you ask for.

CYBERSPACE

Originally from the novel *Neuromancer* by William Gibson, the word cyberspace has been adapted for use with the Internet. It means a virtual 3D world which is made of electronic data that can be seen, touched and heard. Interestingly, the book that coined the catch phrase of the digital age was written on a mechanical typewriter.

DOMAIN NAMES

Once upon a time people had to look for things on the Internet by typing in a funny number called an 'IP Address' that looked a bit like this: 202.139.242.40. Every website had a different number and you'd have to remember them all – it was an impossible task. But then, some very clever person invented the Domain Name, a sort of cover that went over the top of the IP address, and used letters and words to represent the numbers. These look a bit like this: *computer.name.type.country*. If we look at the example *www.microsoft.com.au* it means that '*www*' stands for the World Wide Web, '*microsoft*' is the name of the company we are looking at, '*com*' means that it is a company rather than a school (*edu*) or government office (*gov*), and '*au*' means that this particular computer is stored in Australia.

EMAIL

An Internet tool that lets you send messages very fast. You just type them in and press a button and your little note pops up on someone's computer on the other side of the world. So that your message knows where to go, you give each message the address of your recipient – for example, *george@isp.com* – '*george*' is the name of the person you want it to go to and '*isp.com*' is the Internet Service Provider or company the person uses.

computer.name.t

HTML (HYPER-TEXT MARK-UP LANGUAGE)

A language which describes the formatting of a Web page (ie: the way the page looks), including the hyper-text links. (See also pages 31 and 140–1 for more details.)

IRC (INTERNET RELAY CHAT)

A communication feature that runs over the Internet, separately from the WWW and email features, that lets you 'talk' or 'chat' to other people using a writing-only based system in real time (a computer term for 'live'). This is different to email, because everything you type is sent *straight away*, sentence by sentence, instead of the whole thing at once. When most people join a chat channel or room, they do it anonymously – letting them take on a whole new personality. It ends up just like a school drama class, with everybody pretending to be someone else!

ISP (INTERNET SERVICE PROVIDER)

(See also page 16.) An ISP, or Internet Service Provider, is the company that provides you with your physical connection to the Internet. In return for this service, you pay them money. Sometimes they offer extra services on top of the basic connection, such as a faster connection, an email address or even extra stuff, 'exclusive' content that other people can't see (like an up-to-date news service, or a chat channel).

JAVA

The dictionary definition (or the closest I could get) for JAVA is ‘a simple object-oriented, distributed, interpreted, robust, secure, architecture neutral, portable, high-performance, multi-threaded, and dynamic language’! If you understood that, you’d realise that it’s a computer programming language which lets you make websites interactive and slightly more visually appealing. Usually new users of the Internet won’t notice JAVA as it is integrated into the content, but it is nice to know what is making things work now and then. When creating websites later on, you might be interested in learning it.

LURKER

A boring person who ‘sits in the background’, listening in to what other people are saying in chat channels. They usually don’t contribute to the conversation and sometimes leave if someone tries to talk to them. Many people like to ‘lurk’ for a while to get a feeling of the tone and style of the channel before they participate.

MUDS, MUSHES, MUSES, MOOS

These are all MUs, ‘Multi-user’ simulations which are like IRC channels where the chatters are players in a virtual environment or game. A good example of ‘cyberspace’, although usually without pictures, only words.

NETIQUETTE

The special set of unpoliced rules that Internet users should abide by, so that they don't annoy or offend other users. One example of this is THAT YOU SHOULDN'T TYPE IN CAPITAL LETTERS UNLESS YOU ARE TRYING TO MAKE A POINT!

NEWBIE

A new user of the Internet, often known to break the common rules of simple Netiquette.

NEWSGROUP

An older part of the Net. The real name for newsgroups is USENET. They let you write a letter and post it to a central store of all the old messages (in this case called a 'discussion'). Other people can then read your letters and reply.

NICKNAME

A nickname (or 'nick' as they are more commonly known) is what people use when they join IRC and MUDs. Some people have hundreds of nicknames complete with their own personalities.

SNAIL MAIL

The opposite of email. It's what you thought mail was, with posties delivering to the front of your house, until you hooked up to the Internet. Compared to the electronic way, this delivery method is about as slow as a snail!

SPEED

No, it's not some illicit substance, but the rate at which data (information) is sent between other computers on the Internet and yours. While this is connected to the amount of bandwidth you have, there are a few other things that can change the 'speed' – the main one being the modem that you have. Modems today are generally made at two speeds: 33.3k, and the faster (but less reliable) 56k.

URL (UNIFORM RESOURCE LOCATER)

An address that points to something on the Internet. Web addresses usually start with http:// and then go on to include the domain name: http:// stands for the section of the Internet that is being used. If you're using Usenet newsgroups, then it would start with news://.

WEBSITE

A collection of pages of information found on the World Wide Web. A website about a band, for example, might have pages about the lead singer, the lyrics to their music, and even sound.

WIZARD

An electronic help tool that guides you through certain problems or activities. An example of a wizard is one that asks you to provide information about yourself such as your hobbies, your address, etc. and then it automatically makes up a personal website with the information you have keyed in. Wizards are often included in computer software, but especially in programs which help you make websites.

WWW

Just another one of those sections of the Internet. Actually, the World Wide Web is one of the most popular at the moment. It's the bit with all the pretty graphics, videos and sound.

¶

connecting to the wired world

I don't think there is much I need to say here about the actual connecting. Computers seem to have a mind of their own – evil minds, intent on destroying you and working only when you want them to turn off. Even the other day (3 years after I first set up a computer successfully for the Net), one of my computers just wouldn't connect, and after a lot of banging my head on the keyboard, and calls to Microsoft technical support all I had to show for an afternoon's work was a nasty red bruise on my forehead. (My Internet connection on that computer still doesn't work properly!)

The most important thing to do is make sure you have everything you need ready before you start, to avoid having to make an unintended rush for some new accessory.

The 3 fundamentals you'll need are:

[a] a computer

[b] a modem and a phone line

[c] an internet service provider

First things first: the computer itself. Just about any type of computer will do – usually the newer the better though. It really depends on what you want to do with it. In general, any computer made after 1995 will be able to handle nearly everything the Internet has to offer with differing levels of success.

After you've got a computer sorted out the next thing you should start shopping around for is an Internet Service Provider. Basically an Internet Service Provider is a company or group of people who do just what their name says – they provide you with your Internet service. They link you up to the network and work in the background to make sure everything's running properly.

what should you expect to be working?

If you are unhappy with the service your ISP is giving you, don't hesitate to complain or even change ISPs if you are still unhappy. You are paying them, you know. Depending on what you pay, you have a right to expect that your ISP will supply you with:

- **A connection to the Internet that you can actually connect to.** Sometimes, because Internet Service Providers want to save money, they don't buy enough equipment for a lot of users to connect at once. This means you'll get a busy signal when you try to log in.

- **A fast connection.** If your connection is meant to be at a certain speed but it seems very slow, visit a friend and try to connect using their provider at your speed. If there is much difference, complain!

- **Good customer service.** The person on the other end of your ISP's help line should be nice and treat you as a customer who is actually paying for something rather than an irritating idiot who is wasting their precious time.

All Tech-Support Lines are busy, please wait for the next...

have a NICE day!

Now these Internet Service Providers don't do this for nothing. In fact, a lot of people who started ISP companies a while back are now very happily driving their truck loads of money to the bank. The prices they charge vary a lot and they are changing all the time, but generally the larger companies charge $3 to $5 for each hour you are on-line, while the smaller ones charge $1 to $3 an hour. The difference is because of the 'extra' services the larger companies say they provide. Probably the best idea is to decide exactly what services you need, how long you plan to spend on-line (remember to triple this number, ready for when you become addicted), and how much money you plan to spend – then shop around until you find one that suits your plan. Remember, you can always change providers.

Two other really, really, really important things you'll need are a telephone line and a modem. I'm sure you're starting to think that whoever makes up these weird words like 'modem' and 'cybersurfing' must have a very imaginative (or strange) mind. Actually a modem turns the digital bits and bytes of information coming out of your computer into analog signals (an old-fashioned way of storing information) that can travel down the phone lines to the ISP who then just passes them along to another computer through telephone lines, and these pass them on to another computer and another and another in a kind of hot potato game along the fastest and most direct route until the information ends up at its destination. Of course a modem can also work the other way – receiving analog signals and turning them into digital instructions your computer can understand.

At the moment the old-fashioned telephone lines are still the most popular method of linking up these computers on the Internet, but they have a major problem. Because they are not designed to handle the big load of new traffic that the Internet causes, they can be **extremely**

SSSSSSLLLLLLOOOOOOOOWWWWWW.

(Well, actually they are super fast – but if I have to wait more than 10 seconds for a page to travel from America, I start to get extremely frustrated.) Soon, more and more people will change to using high capacity cables that are designed with computers and the Internet in mind.

If these cables are available in your area, and you can afford the rather hefty price tag, then I suggest you try hooking up with one of these. It's well worth it in terms of speed and everyone will be using them sooner or later.

cable providers

The best place to find out about these is your local cable TV or phone company.

Currently one of the most popular cable providers is the @Home network, which provides high speed access to lots of cities in the US and Canada. Their website is at http://www.home.com.

In Australia, Telstra is currently the only operator of a cable service (see http://www.telstra.com.au). In the UK, *Cable and Wireless Communications* are one of the biggest providers (their website is at http://www.cwc.com/main.html.).

The Cable Modem University keeps a very complete database of information regarding high speed Internet services at http://www.catv.org/modem/frame/deploy.html.

Japan, Canada and France have services up and running, although New Zealand is yet to come on-line.

A **basic modem** runs at **28.8bps** or **33.3bps** speed (bps stands for 'Bits Per Second'), while many run **slower** and some **faster**. A **special cable modem** is needed for those high speed things I mentioned above.

what else do you need?

Well, those are the basics – the rest really depends on what you want to use the Internet for. You will also need some software including:

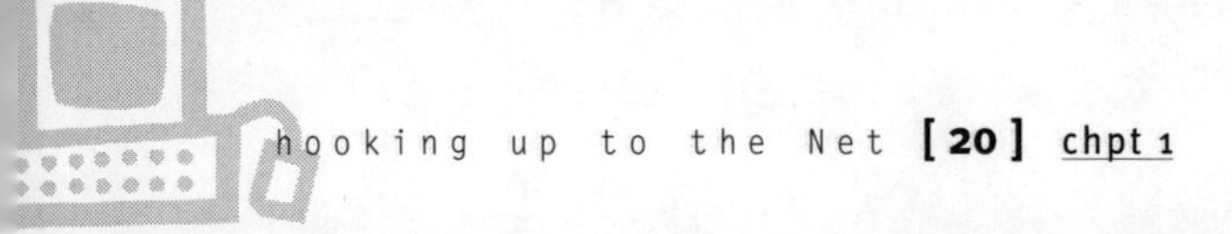

WINSOCK A CONNECTION PROGRAM THAT COMMUNICATES WITH YOUR MODEM TO DIAL UP YOUR INTERNET SERVICE PROVIDER. ONCE YOU ARE CONNECTED, IT WORKS WITH YOUR ISP'S COMPUTER TO TELL THEM THAT YOU HAVE LOGGED IN AND THAT THEY SHOULD START CHARGING YOU! WINSOCK NOW COMES LOADED WITH WINDOWS 95/98, AND THERE IS AN EQUIVALENT FOR THE MACOS.

NETSCAPE NAVIGATOR (NOW PART OF A 'SET' OF SOFTWARE CALLED COMMUNICATOR) OR **MICROSOFT INTERNET EXPLORER**, USED FOR BROWSING THE WORLD WIDE WEB.

Usually a collection of Internet software is supplied by your Internet Service Provider when you first join up. However, if you need more once you're on-line, the best place is The Ultimate Collection of Winsock Software (or TUCOWS). Their website address is http://www.tucows.com.

There are also plenty of accessories available – from virtual reality glasses to video cameras, sound cards and speakers. You could spend a fortune stocking up on Net goodies. These add to your overall experience and might make your time on-line just that little bit more enjoyable – although for the price, maybe you could live without them . . .

That's about it from me about connecting (I don't want this to be a boring manual). So if you need more help setting up your Net connection I've included a list of great books on page 165. ¶

THE ADVENTURES OF

CYBERGRRL

life after

chapter 2 connection

you're on-line!

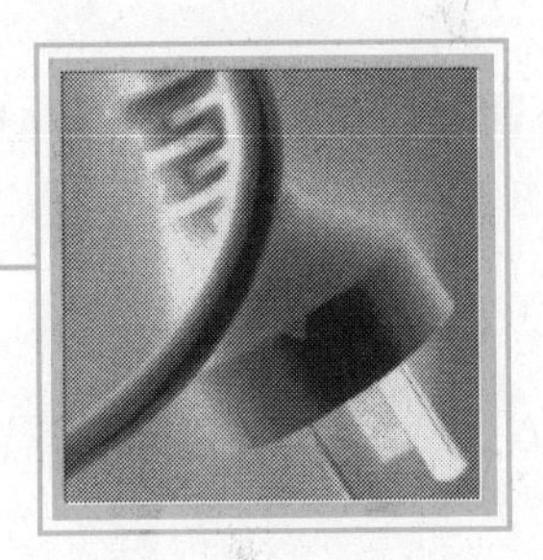

Wow! So you're connected. After (usually) much frustration and cursing at your computer your Internet set-up is complete. You're on-line! As Trekkies would say, you are about to enter a new frontier and 'boldly go where . . .' Oh well, you know what I mean . . .

Now that you're connected and can get on the Internet, it may all seem very confusing. But it's not. I'll explain the basic things you'll need to know on your Internet journey.

When you open up your World Wide Web browser, a page will pop up. This is usually the default start page set by either your Internet Service Provider or the maker of your software. These are there to advertise their own products, or to act as a useful jumping-off point for your Internet travels. It's lucky you can set it to go to whatever you want pretty easily: if you type in say, 'Spice Girls' or 'Teletubbies', you'll find a variety of official and unofficial sites.

WRONG WAY GO BACK

addresses

BEWARE newbies next 1km

100% Official Teletubby Information Centre **http://www.teletubby.co.uk/teletubbyland.html**

The address of the page will usually be written somewhere up the top of the screen. In most browser software it looks like a little box where you can type things. Normally these things you type in are called URLs and start with **http://**. To change the address you just have to type a new address into that box and press enter. Other ways of displaying the information available on the Internet are becoming available now, and in the future these could replace the trusty browser. One of these is 'push and pull' – sounds a bit weird, but all it does is display Internet information on your operating system (such as Windows or Mac). This would mean that you don't actually have to click and search around for information – the program just gets some and serves it up to you – a bit like television. Personally I don't see the point. If they are going to make something just like TV, then why don't we forget the Internet ever happened and go back to the good old box? Stooopid! Today, the browser companies have got in on the act (so they don't just become insignificant nobodies), and

Lost?

superhighway 6km

you'll now find 'push' technology sold as part of Netscape Communicator or Internet Explorer.

http:// ???

Every place on the Internet has an address, which you need to be able to get anywhere. These start with http:// which stands for 'Hyper-text transfer protocol'. If we just go back to my car idea for a second (no, I'm not particularly interested in motor sports, but thanks for asking . . .), http:// is a bit like the engine used to power the car. It processes all your requests and instructions, puts them together and produces something in return. In a car this would be called movement, but in terms of the Internet it's information: http is what **makes the Web work.** When combined with a domain name to create a website address, http:// is called a URL, or Uniform Resource Locater.

superhighway 30m

ENOUGH TUTORIALS – LET'S GO SOMEWHERE!

If you don't know any particular sites on the World Wide Web, the best place to start is a Web Search Engine or Directory (the new buzz word is 'portal'). Currently there are quite a few Search Engines on the Internet and they all say they are better than each other. Working out which ones are telling the truth is the hard bit. At the moment two of the most popular are Hotbot and Altavista.

UltimateMegaSuperExcellentSearcher™
"It will find Anything and Everything."℠

Go to the Altavista site at

http://www.altavista.digital.com

by clicking inside the address box at the top. Delete any current address, and replace it with the address for Altavista – press enter once and you're done.

While you're thinking of a topic to search for, I'll explain a bit about these Search Engines. They work by going around the Web and copying information on all the sites they visit into huge databases or collections of information which they let you search. It's all free because they display advertising – a bit like commercial television. Search Engines are very popular – some get more than 30 million visits a day.

Anyway, back to Altavista. You just type what you want to find out about in the box, using key words, and press 'search'. Within a couple of seconds another page should load with the results of your search. These are ordered in some particular way – but don't ask me what it is (you can sometimes get

some pretty weird entries appearing in your results!). All you have to do now is click on the coloured (and usually underlined) writing (also usually blue) and you'll be taken to the site of your choice. It's that easy! You'll be a pro in no time.

The blue writing you just clicked on is called a 'hyperlink'. But people are lazy so they now seem to be called 'links'. These links are your 'bridges' around the WWW. Clicking on something that's hyperlinked (sounds a bit like a disease) will always do something or take you somewhere else.

Some other Internet Search Engines are:

<u>Hotbot</u> **http://www.hotbot.com**
<u>Anzwers</u> **http://www.anzwers.com.au**
<u>Webcrawler</u> **http://www.webcrawler.com**
<u>Lycos</u> **http://www.lycos.com**
<u>Excite</u> **http://www.excite.com**

These work in the same way as Altavista, but the difference is in the size of their databases. Some are bigger, some are smaller. Bigger does not always mean better, because often a big database just has a lot more junk.

A good place to begin for any search is an Internet Directory. They won't find you nearly as much information on a topic – but what they will find will usually be more useful, and much better organised. These are different to Search Engines because they do not automatically go around collecting every bit of information they find. Instead they wait for people to submit the information to them by filling out a form. Like all websites, you get to these Internet Directories by typing in a URL in the address box at the top of the screen.

The 'king' of the Internet Directory world is Yahoo!. Yahoo! was basically just a group of friends and their page of 'links', which they began just as the Internet was starting to get noticed. Within a couple of months this 'page of links' was worth hundreds of millions of dollars. Yahoo! is a great tool and I use it all the time.

Yahoo! also has a younger brother called Yahooligans!. This is a directory of sites designed only for kids who are 8 to 14 years old. You can search Yahoo! or just 'browse' by categories such as the Arts, Computers and the Internet, Reference, etc, etc . . .

If you are really **stuck** trying to find a site worth visiting there are many sites on the Internet ready to suggest one, such as the Cool Site of the Day. Happy Surfing!

addresses

Altavista **http://www.altavista.digital.com**
Yahoo! **http://www.yahoo.com**
Yahooligans! **http://www.yahooligans.com**
Cool Site of the Day **http://cool.infi.net**

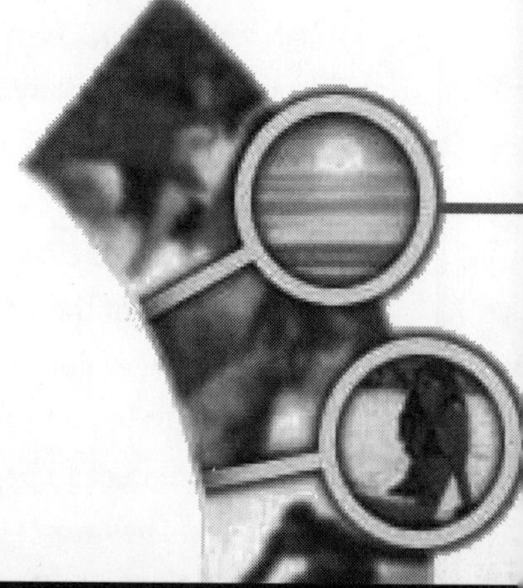

THE WET SURFING PA
http://surf.to/twsp/

the king of links

As I mentioned, the 'King' of all Internet search tools is Yahoo!. So what does that make Jerry Yang, the co-creator of Yahoo!? Your Roving Reporter asked him a few questions:

Your Roving Reporter: When did you first get onto the Net? What were your first impressions?

Jerry Yang: I've been on the Net since I was in college in the late 80s. The Internet didn't take off as a commercial medium till 1993, so the early days were used as mainly an academic and research medium. I always was very impressed with the potential of the Net, and believed from very early on that it would impact millions of people.

YRR: So you just took it upon yourselves to catalogue the Net? What made you do it? (Seems like a long and boring task to me . . .)

JY: My partner, co-founder of Yahoo!, David Filo and I really thought the Net was an interesting place, and all kinds of unique content was being generated. We felt that if the Internet continued to grow, it would ultimately need something like a Yahoo! catalogue to make it useful and easy for people. We just continued to catalogue the Web because it was fun and amazing to watch the Web grow. In retrospect it was great to be part of the explosiveness of the Web!

YRR: In the early days, did you ever think that it was just too much work and consider giving up?

JY: The work was very tough sometimes, and we got tired and were sometimes unsure of where this may all lead. But I don't think we ever thought about giving up – the truth is, we were having too much fun!

YRR: When did you realise that you had started what was to become one of the most popular Internet sites, and a Net leading brand?

JY: I guess when we started as a company in April 1995, we realised that we had some pretty good brand recognition, and realised that if we were to execute well as a business, we'd be in good shape to be an influence on the Internet.

YRR: How did Yahoo! find enough cash to continue as a commercial company?

JY: We raised our first round through venture capitalists [these are people who invest money in high-tech companies they think will make a fortune – YRR] – a firm called Sequoia Capital. We subsequently raised more money through corporate investors and partners.

YRR: Yahoo! has been concentrating on content services [their own information, instead of just links to others' information – YRR] over the past year or so. Is that correct? What is ahead for Yahoo! in the future? Will you bring in more and more content – and not be 'just a search tool'?

JY: I think we will continue to change our service as the demands of our users change – that's the key to our success so far and will continue to be the way we grow. I think, as you suggest, the content will be more important for us – but we've also begun to focus on commerce (buying stuff on the Net), and community (email, chat, etc). All of those things are extremely important for the Web to continue to be a big part of people's lives, and that's where I'd like Yahoo! to be useful as well.

YRR: So you've started a billion dollar company . . . What's next for Jerry 'Yahoo' Yang?

JY: I'd like to be at Yahoo!, helping out as long as possible. I'm happy being part of Yahoo!'s growth, and feel that there is still so much potential in where Yahoo! can go.

YRR: Do you think the Net will survive into the future as a research tool without even more complex cataloguing systems . . . I mean, it's very hard to find things now???

JY: I think the technology and software will continue to improve – so yes, I believe that the Net will need to come up with even more complex, and more importantly, user-friendly cataloguing systems to make sense of information for the users.

YRR: Just quickly, do you prefer Netscape or Microsoft's browsers? On features and on principles?

JY: I actually like – and use – both. My feeling is that as long as there are competitive products out there, the users end up benefiting. So as long as they are competing to develop the best for the users, we all win . . . ¶

Sorry folks, just had to slip in that last question . . . !

search! lost? surf ····> discover . . . an experiment in Net crawling

AIM:

To document an example of 'surfing' on the Net.

MATERIALS:

Yahoo!, the words 'lost dogs', and quite a bit of time.

RESULTS:

Thinking how stupid I am, I logged into Yahoo! and typed in **'lost dogs'**. 31 websites **(http://search.aunz.yahoo.com/search/aunz?p=lost+dogs&y=y)**. Strange what some people spend their time on.

So I clicked on Dogs in Canada Needing Homes **(http://www.cyberus.ca/~pfoley/)** just to see what I could find out. Big mistake . . .

IED TOP SECRET

Along with pictures of 'Annelise Vom Eichenbaum [*that's the dog*] with Dad' [*that's the human*], the site has a number of links to other exciting canine locations. So I clicked on one:

LASSIFIED TOP SECRET

dogmark.
presents

Dog Ownership Responsibility **(http://www.king.igs.net/~brica/)**. This site must be pretty good, because it won the 'Cool Dog Site of the Day' award. Wow.

Here I was at the Dogmark site **(http://www.st.rim.or.jp/~ito/d/dogmark.html)** that actually gives out the awards. And what an impressive site it is. Voting, Submit Your Own, Chat - even a couple of links. So guess what I did?

Click.

What I clicked on was a banner ad for 'Dog Treats'. This took me to The Country Butcher **(http://www.countrybutcher.com/)**. Now I was well and truly lost - unless this is where they send the lost dogs? Large Knuckles, Small Rib-bones, Puppy Sausages, Pork Skin Chops, and even something called a Mega Sampler. McDonalds for dogs. Help!

COOL DOG SIT
OF
THE DAY

The Home Vet **(http://www.homevet.com)** is 'helping our beloved pets live longer and happier lives'. And good on them, too. It's not often enough we see people in our society stand up and lend a hand to those in need (especially when they only have paws).

the world's
coolest site
you can walk with

Click.

I feel like a bit of further reading, so am now buying a book at Amazon **http://www.amazon.com/exec/obidos/ASIN/0895778394/qid=904048643/sr=1-2/002-5512763-2052803)**, which The Home Vet (bless his/her heart) kindly linked directly for me. It's called *The Perfect Puppy*, and should be exciting (and I don't even have a dog).

Surfing Amazon.com is something that should be reserved for rainy afternoons. Obviously I could

Click. Click. Click.

for ever and ever. But I actually do have something of a life and looking up dog sites isn't usually part of it.

Your Roving Reporter signing off.

Related site:

Yahoo! Dogs **http://www.yahoo.com.au/Business and Economy/Companies/Animals/Dogs/**

THE ADVENTURES OF CYBERGRRL

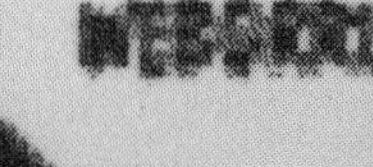

virtual

RMIT
STATE SCHOOL
GRADE 3B
1985

chapter III learning

an electronic reference tool

'there's the bell . . . !'

Some people think that because you use the Internet your **school work** will become worse and you won't do your **homework**. Actually the Internet can make your homework much, much better – and easier too! Here's how . . .

The Internet is really one huge electronic reference tool. The WWW is almost every newspaper article you could ever want, almost every book you could ever read, and just about every picture or map you could ever hope to find.

Why spend hours in the school library searching by hand the limited resources and probably not finding as much, when you can just use the Internet? And it's all electronically searchable. Of course not **everything** in the library is on-line, but plenty of more obscure items which can't be found in the average-middle-of-the-road school, **can** be found on-line. **BUT,** when using the Internet for school work it's best not to place complete trust in it. It's great for some things, like looking up information for a project on aliens or soil regeneration, but the information you will find is generally much more specialised and not nearly as readable. Often the best stuff is created by and for 'experts', and it takes a bit of background knowledge to even understand what they are talking about. The Internet might help to raise your grades from B to A+, but it won't replace the traditional resources – yet. However, if it's 11 o'clock at night and a project is due the next day, while you are still thinking of a possible topic – well, that is when it really comes in handy (!!!).

And what lots of people don't remember is the best thing of all: if the WWW is a good way of getting to lots of information written by experts, then **email is the perfect way of communicating directly with the experts.** The Internet was once (during part of its very varied life) a tool used mainly by researchers and teachers to share information. This means that there are experts in just about everything on-line, ready for you to contact them with a list of questions. Literally a whole world of information is available, especially through the university contact pages, and mailing

lists. For example, many lecturers and professors have their own homepages you can look up and contact for the latest developments in their field of research.

networked school

First of all, here are some great sites to try:

HOMEWORK HELPER

http://www.homeworkhelper.com

This service of the 'Electronic Library' is amazing. You just have to enter a question and it'll bring up all the documents related to your question. It's like having your own personal library and librarian. There are over 2000 books, as well as TV and radio scripts and millions of newspapers, maps and pictures. It does cost money, but could well be worthwhile.

SCHOOL WORK

http://www.schoolwork.org

School Work is run by a library and has lots of links to help people with homework on plenty of subjects.

PROJECT GUTENBERG

http://www.gutenberg.org

Project Gutenberg has a target of getting 10,000 full-text copies of famous, out-of-copyright books on-line by the year

2000. While there are at least 1000 on-line now, they are incredibly useful if it is the night before some huge project is due and you need a copy of a book in a rush!

Once again, Yahoo! might be the best place to start because it is quite specific and can find much more reliable, 'quality' sites.

when school sucks . . .

Does the statement 'You never have to do homework again' sound good? It certainly does to me. This ingenious (or devious) plan is the idea of a number of clever webmasters across the globe, who also happen to be students.

This is how it works: when you do a project that gets a pretty good mark, you send it to the webmaster who puts it on the site – making it freely available for downloading by anyone. Other people do the same thing until there is quite a collection of book reviews, reports and essays on topics as diverse as History, Science, Mathematics, Law, Geography and Art. Next time you're stuck for homework you're supposed to just download a project someone else has submitted and hand it in to your teacher – and he or she (supposedly) won't even know the difference.

But, however negatively they are portrayed at Kenny Sahr's School Sucks website, teachers aren't all that dumb and many now check the site to see what is on offer (and if it matches up with any of their own students' work).

Ironically, it's the very controversy surrounding School Sucks which has transformed it into one of the most popular sites on the Internet. Kenny describes it as 'a combination

of eager students, angry professors and a curious media'. If Your Roving Reporter counts as media, then he certainly ***is*** curious . . .

Since being reported in over 500 newspapers and magazines across the US, Kenny's School Sucks has had to change. Instead of being a complete homework resource, School Sucks now advertises itself as a place to get sample essays and book references so you can go off and **write one yourself!**

In fact Kenny does suggest that the writing in School Sucks is so bad that the website has turned into a political weapon to prove what a terrible job the US education system is doing – much to the dislike of the teachers. Sahr shares a motto with author Mark Twain, 'Never let your schooling interfere with your education', and School Sucks users tend to agree. 'Schoolsucks.com is a really cool site! How would the world live without it?', asks one!

A quick-witted teacher goes in for the kill:

It's also very ironic that you crusade as a person who wants to ensure equal access to information, and yet the quality of the papers on your website is really appalling. You're taking advantage of people who don't know any better. Why? Your personal web page tells it all, with those don't-I-look-ravishing photographs. Ahh, snake-oil salesmen and self-promoters.

To which Kenny quickly replies:

> These papers are sent in by students. They are reflective of the students in this country and are the results of YOUR work. If these papers suck, YOU suck.

Perhaps Joshua Quittner in *Time* magazine has the right idea:

> I can't believe, frankly, that I'm writing about him too. I mean, it's just so wrong.

So, it might be best if you forget about Kenny and his devious schemes to prop up the United States education system. After all, the **primary aim of all this is to cheat**. Hmm . . . in fact, I'm sick of Kenny and the whole School Sucks idea. If some people can write their own essays, then why can't everyone? I'm **almost** sick of him – but not quite. As Joshua and Kenny well know, it's just too good a story!

School Sucks **http://www.schoolsucks.com/main.html**

can the Web be trusted?

As you now know, the Internet truly is an **amazing place**. There is **so much** information available. In fact, the Internet ***is* information**. **But is it** information you can ***trust***?

If you read something in a book we tend to believe it – well, most of us do. This is because it has been checked by people we assume are responsible publishers, editors and writers. Anyway, why would anyone bother writing a non-fiction reference book that wasn't true? No one would buy it. The Internet, however, is different. First of all, people don't usually **buy** information from the Internet – it's already free and in the 'public domain'. Secondly, responsible publishers aren't usually involved. Everything on the Internet is just as easy to get to as everything else – and just about anybody and his/her dog/cat can publish on it easily. So how can we trust it? Well, the simple answer is we **can't**.

seeing IS NOT believing

Chuck Farnham's Weird World is one example of a site that the word truth might or might not apply to – you can't be sure. The site says, for example, that a picture of some guy in the back of an ambulance is Kurt Cobain. It also has transcripts from the black box recorder of the Challenger Space Shuttle and Nicole Brown Simpson's 'help' telephone calls. It is all very interesting to read, but I wouldn't advise you to use it in your next school project.

This situation will change over time as more of those 'responsible publishers' get connected and set up information sites of their own. Until then, the Net will be an important and useful resource that you ***just can't necessarily trust***. But don't let this stop you using it as a resource – first-hand accounts and 'different angles' on many issues can be found on-line. It isn't a replacement for other resources, but a new kind of resource itself.

addresses

__**Chuck Farnham's Weird World**__ **http://monkey.hooked.net/monkey/m/chuck/**

ready, aim . . . peacefire!

After five minutes on the Net, you'll realise that **censorship** is one **hot topic.**

Should we be allowed to see . . . well, let's say 'undesirable' things (get the idea?) and if no, then who or what should be blocking our access? One idea was to make a program that works with your Internet browser (such as Netscape) to block out these unwanted sites. But how do these work? That's the problem. Some of these programs, including a product called CYBERsitter, have a 'ban list' – a list of sites that are blocked. The thing is that they won't tell you what's on this list, and CYBERsitter, in my opinion, has blocked access to some perfectly okay sites.

Safe Kids Online
www.safekids.com

So, in steps Peacefire, the teen-net anti-censorship alliance. This organisation (members have an average age of 16) spreads information about the blocking programs, and also participates in legal action against the software companies who create them – calling for the banning of these 'ban'

programs, citing the First Amendment to the US constitution, which gives all US citizens the right to free speech. Once again, Your Roving Reporter took time out to ask Peacefire founder Bennett Haselton some questions:

Your Roving Reporter: When did you get onto the Net?

Bennett Haselton: August 1995, when I first got to University. Love at first sight.

YRR: How did you become interested in civil rights?

BH: I started reading about the Communications Decency Act in June-July 1996 and thinking that minors were getting shafted in the proposed 'solutions' to the problem. I did most of my research from computers at my summer job. Most of the time, I was probably supposed to be working. So it's a good thing they weren't using any monitor software on me.

YRR: So you think self-censorship is the key?

BH: No, I think that for people to censor what they say is one of the worst forms of censorship, because it happens as a result of being 'intimidated' by the government, rather than directly threatened. That makes it a lot harder to fight in court, since you can't fight 'intimidation' without proving it first.

That assumes that you were talking about people censoring what they 'say', producing 'cleaned-up' versions of their websites for public consumption. If you mean people censoring what they 'see', by choosing whether or not to go to a particular website, then of course we hope people will take matters into their own hands that way.

YRR: Do you see Peacefire expanding to other aspects of the infringement of civil rights (on the Net)?

BH: Probably not, since our emphasis is more on the violation of minors' rights than on the violation of cyber-rights. So although there is talk of expanding Peacefire's role to include a broader youth-rights agenda, we probably won't expand into other areas of Internet activism, such as crypto advocacy [the campaign for easier access to strong security technology – YRR] or the copyright debate.

YRR: You have obviously been very clever in your use of the media to attract attention towards Peacefire. Do you think the fact that the average age of Peacefire members is 16 helped this?

BH: I think it has had an effect on the way people view, for example, the feud between us and CYBERsitter. Whether that's for good or for bad in the long term, it's hard to tell. Certainly in the short term it helps the story to go further whenever something newsworthy happens between us and CYBERsitter. In the long term I wonder about the good that it does, because so many people who write in seem to treat us like children, or, to be more accurate, treat us the way that some adults think children ought to be treated.

YRR: What are your plans for the future?

BH: I think that before too long there will be a legal controversy over a public institution, such as a public library or state school, using blocking software, and a lawsuit might be filed. While we don't have the resources to fund our own lawsuit, I'm hoping that we can play an important role by contributing information and expertise on the blocking software issue.

Peacefire **http://www.peacefire.org**

Of course, it should also be said that there are sometimes some very good reasons why adults are asking for more censorship on the Internet, especially where young children are concerned (and Internet users are getting younger every day!). The issue of access is one of the real concerns for every user of the Internet.

SCHOOL WORK AND THE INTERNET: some useful helpers . . .

Australian Federal Government Entry Point

http://www.fed.gov.au/

Goodies galore here. Actually, it's amazing how much useful information the government stores on its endless web servers scattered around the place. Links provide pathways to just about every government department and agency, including Employment, Education, Health, Environment and Foreign Affairs. Information on how the government works and the different people involved can also be found here if you look hard enough, plus up-to-date information on current government enquiries, parliamentary sittings, etc. A wealth of info is here for school projects and just general interest! **The Source (http://www.thesource.gov.au/)** is a government created site designed to fulfil every Youth wish on such exciting topics as Staying Healthy, Alcohol and Drugs, Juvenile Justice, and (drum roll) Road Safety. Just what I spend my time looking up on the Net! Very worthwhile – if you feel like walking out in front of a car . . .

The CSIRO

http://www.csiro.au/

If you are looking for science-related information, the CSIRO is a one-stop shop. For example, I got some info on Land Management for a Geography project and downloaded a video on plastic wood (oxymoron alert!). You'll notice it's so important it doesn't even need a .gov domain name.

The Australian Bureau of Statistics

http://www.abs.gov.au/

Wow – 8,608.2 people were newly employed in Australia in August 1998. And 64,902 new cars were bought in May! These and many other exciting facts and figures are available at the Bureau of Statistics. And it made me think: what kind of person actually bothers to work this stuff out? Must be a terrible job going around and counting all those people. 1 person, 2 persons, 3 persons, 4 persons, 5 persons, etc. all day. And then it made me think: what kind of person actually needs to know about it?!

NASA

http://www.nasa.gov

Even if you don't plan on being an astronaut at some stage in the future, it's hard not to find something interesting at the NASA site, which includes information on all the latest missions, and squillions of photos and images of assorted extra-terrestrial places. There is even a section dealing with good old planet Earth.

The Natural History Museum, London

http://www.nhm.ac.uk/

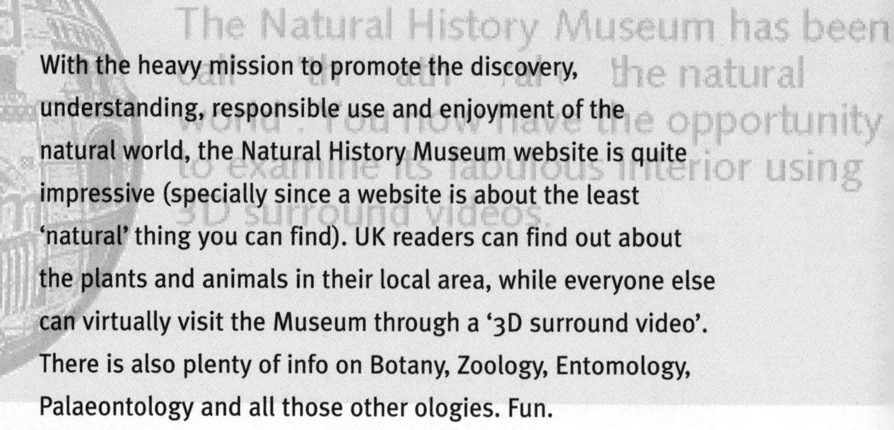

With the heavy mission to promote the discovery, understanding, responsible use and enjoyment of the natural world, the Natural History Museum website is quite impressive (specially since a website is about the least 'natural' thing you can find). UK readers can find out about the plants and animals in their local area, while everyone else can virtually visit the Museum through a '3D surround video'. There is also plenty of info on Botany, Zoology, Entomology, Palaeontology and all those other ologies. Fun.

The National Archives of New Zealand

http://www.archives.govt.nz/

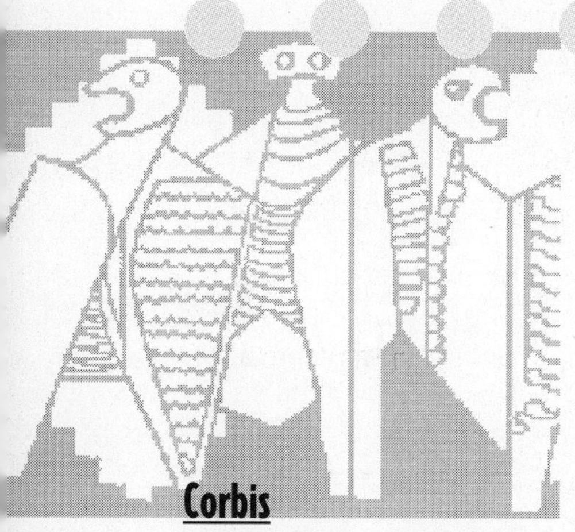

The NZ Archives are the 'Keeper of the Public Record – the Memory of Government'. I'm not sure exactly how this happens (a human brain in a glass jar connected to a computer was the first thing that came to mind . . . yes, call me sick), but it seems they have quite a few things important enough to remember. It's nice that they do that anyway, because it means people like Your Roving Reporter don't have to bother. If you're looking into NZ history, this is the place to go.

Corbis

http://www.corbis.com

Some people think a picture tells a thousand words. Personally, I don't think pictures can speak – but that aside, if you're looking for an image of **anything** look no further than Corbis. I typed in a couple of things – witches, lemon trees and the Mona Lisa – and came up with great electronic images of each (and a number of extras I never expected).

Did you know that you can . . . ?

addresses

- order archival info material on lots of topics from the government itself?
- look up historical photos and other exhibitions from the State Library of Victoria, and elsewhere, on the Net?
- chat about your maths homework with people around the world at sites like Algebra Online?
- participate in a question-and-answer forum with all your Shakespeare queries?
- look at any point on earth from space (well, actually from your computer)?

State Library of Victoria http://www.slv.vic.gov.au
Algebra Online http://www.algebra-online.com/
Shakespearean Homework Helper http://members.aol.com/liadona2/shakespeare.html
Global View from Space http://sdcd.gsfc.nasa.gov/ISTO/dro/global/menuq.html

politics and the Net

When Your Roving Reporter was racking his brains to come up with a way to describe Senator Natasha Stott Despoja, he came across the 'Natasha Stott Despoja Fan Page' created by uni student Ross Chapman, who says:

'The thing about Natasha Stott Despoja is that she is a spunk. Alluring. Appealing. Attractive. Delectable. Desirable. Sexy. Lush. Intriguing. Ravishing. Sensual. Bewitching. Captivating. Enchanting. Impressive. And basically completely irresistible.'

Who said people don't like politicians? However, on a serious note, Natasha, at 28, is the youngest member of the Australian Federal Parliament, and the Deputy Leader of the Australian Democrats. She is responsible for, among other things, Information Technology and Youth Affairs.

Your Roving Reporter: Hi Natasha – so when did you first get on to the Net?

NSD: 1996.

YRR: And what did you use it for?

NSD: Emails!!!

YRR: Do you think that Internet use might change the nature of politics?

NSD: Yes. I tabled the first-ever Internet petition in the Parliament. I see it opening up another democratic channel – through emails to members and through petitions.

YRR: But what happens if some people in the community don't have access to this technology?

NSD: Of course there remain barriers to access on the information superhighway – not everyone has equal access to information technology, let alone the money for computers, lessons, etc. One of our jobs as decision-makers promoting IT should be to ensure that people are not locked out of such technology due to financial and other constraints such as age or disability.

YRR: So you think IT enhances the ability of people to participate in a democracy.

NSD: Well, as for Internet petitions – while this may appeal only to a certain section of people, I believe it is opening up a new channel – not preventing others from accessing the age-old petitioning process, but actually encouraging people, maybe who have never thought of it before, to contact the parliament or even their local member. A lot of the people who email me say that it is the first time they have contacted a pollie and they would not normally do it through the usual channels – snail mail, phone, lobbying, meetings, etc . . .

YRR: Have you ever tried Internet Chat?

NSD: No, but my mum who has just discovered the Internet is mad keen!

Sites:

Australian Democrats **http://www.democrats.org.au**

The NSD Fan Page **http://hex.arts.unimelb.edu.au/~rac/nsd/**

§potlight on

chapter 4 entertainment

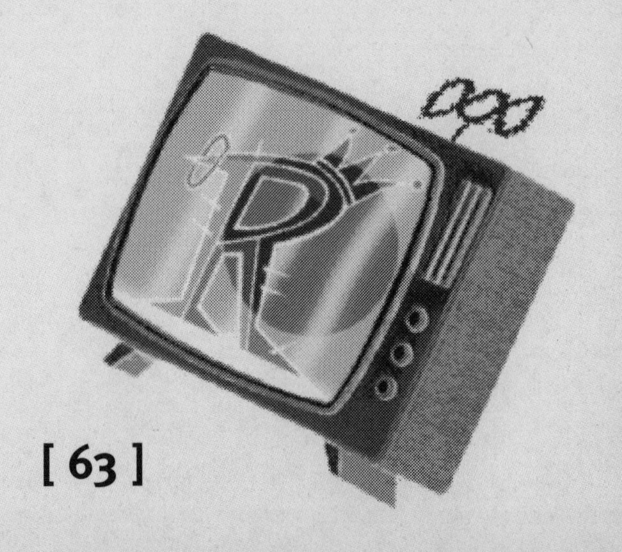

Satire: When a joke is best!

satire: when a joke is best!

When is Microsoft not Microsoft? Usually when it's a parody of the Microsoft website. These clever sites are popping up around the place quite often now, their creators priding themselves on their wit and wisdom. Ever since companies started putting up major sites on the Web, there has been someone to point out all the faults. Some site parodies are just meant to be funny, while others are more serious self - labelled 'hate' pages. ¶

The Microsnot site was one of my favourites (unfortunately no longer available, but a great example of the type of thing to look for) and used a lot of graphics copied from the Microsoft website. The page looked so much like the official Microsoft page that you could get confused, and called itself 'Microsnot: the World Leader in Hype'. The site had everything including press releases. In one, Microsnot announced that it had acquired England and that it had made some changes to the licence agreement for a product called English (now a Microsnot trademark):

"**English**™ will no longer be made available on a Public Domain basis. All users of English™ must register with **Microsnot**. A trial version of English™ will be made available with a **limited vocabulary.**"

Other sites can be much harsher, such as the 'Why AOL Sucks' site. This page explains in detail why they think AOL, um . . . 'sucks'. If you haven't yet had the privilege of finding out, AOL stands for America Online and is the biggest Internet Service Provider in the world: the fact that so many people use it must count for something.

Sites such as these bring up a whole new problem – the problem of free speech. Many of these really go the whole way, defaming the companies and people on the receiving end. For example, the 'Micro$oft hate page' had a picture of Bill Gates about to be blown apart with a pump-action rifle!

Even scarier are the people who have almost evil beliefs. They've realised that the Internet provides one of the last pretty much uncensored public areas for them to voice their strong and controversial opinions. A crowd of Nazis and terrorists have put up websites.

Whether people should be allowed to say things like this on the Internet is a bit of a media favourite at the moment – although I don't think it is nearly as much of a problem as they make it out to be. Just like all the other beat-ups about the Internet, it'll soon calm down. People will probably lose interest. And maybe those hate spreaders will realise that there is more to do in life than just having a go at everyone else.

Meanwhile, the legitimate satires are just too funny to close:

addresses

Why America Online Sucks **http://www.aolsucks.org**
Micro$oft Hate Page **http://www.enemy.org**

Other Web parodies to have a look at:

Thanks a Billion **http://www.jwp.bc.ca/saulm/ii/thanks.htm**
Microsoff **http://www.jwp.bc.ca/saulm/ii/ms.htm**
These two sites are very clever. The first takes a new angle on the 'Ask Bill' column in the New York Times and other papers, where imaginary people ask Bill to share his wealth. Microsoff is a parody of the Microsoft website organised in a similar style to Microsnot.

Netape **http://www.bcpl.lib.md.us/~dbroida/netape.html**
A parody of the Netscape homepage.

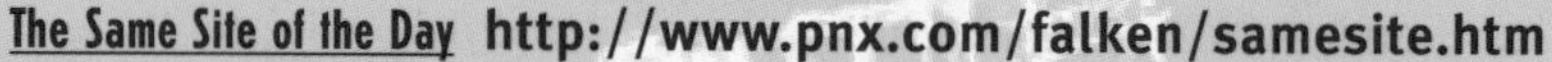

The Same Site of the Day **http://www.pnx.com/falken/samesite.htm**

If you're getting sick of those Cool Site of the Day/Month/Hour, etc. that are appearing all over the Web at an alarming rate, the Same Site of the Day is a refreshing change (maybe they aren't the best words). The Same Site of the Day's promise is to give you a site that is 'just as cool as the day before'.

Stale **http://www.stale.com**

A parody of the Slate popular culture e-zine (the Internet equivalent of a printed magazine) which, as its name suggests, is always out of date.

looking at the world through the Web

I've noticed that some people become addicted to the Net. They can't stop being connected to the screen! In fact, an odd phenomenon seems to be happening – for instance, instead of actually going out and buying a fish tank with some real live fish in it to look at, these Net addicts just type in a Web address and visit a virtual camera.

I'm going to call this occurrence the 'looking at the world through the Web' phenomenon, and it's getting a large number of fans who seem to think that just because you *can* have a video camera hooked up to your computer, feeding images of the view from your second-storey window all over the world, that you *should*.

The weird thing is that no one seems to have realised that they should be putting cameras in mildly interesting places. The only Web camera that I've heard was put to any useful

location was one that took pictures of a volcano in New Zealand as it was erupting. The obvious advantages of using technology for remote viewing of events of scientific interest are . . . well . . . obvious.

If you're one of those kinds of people who listen to the weather report instead of going outside, you might find the following sites a good start to totally sealing yourself off from the outside world.

Yahoo! – Devices Attached to the Web **http://www.yahoo.com/Computers_and_Internet/Internet/Interesting_Devices_Connected_to_the_Net/**
A long list of sites that is sure to keep you busy for many a day, looking out of windows, into offices, houses, fish tanks, garages, hotels, streets, gardens, etc, etc, etc, etc, etc.

Surfcam **http://live.ninemsn.com.au/surfcam/default.asp**
No longer do intrepid Australian surfers have to wake up early and battle down to the beach simply to find the 10 metre wave: the one you suspect is little more than a puddle. Simply check Surfcam, a service operated free of charge to webbed folk, allowing them a view of the conditions on a 'try before you buy basis'. At least it finally gives some meaning to 'surfing the Web'.

Interactive Model Railway **http://rr-vs.infomatik.uni-ulm.de/rrbin/ui/RRPage.html**
The Interactive Model Railway has taken the 'Looking at the world through the Web' phenomenon one step further and made it the 'Looking at and participating in the world through the Web'. You can actually move the train around tracks and watch it as it goes. This is one site I do find really fascinating.

addresses

Steve's Wearable Wireless Cam **http://wearcam.org/**

Until recently Steve walked around with a camera attached to his head that sent a signal back to his computer. Although this little project in 'camera connectivity' is put on hold while he's out of town, it's still a very interesting stop-over and makes you realise the full potential (and limits) of this technology. If there's one question I'd like to ask it'd be, 'What happens when the transmitter moves out of range?'.

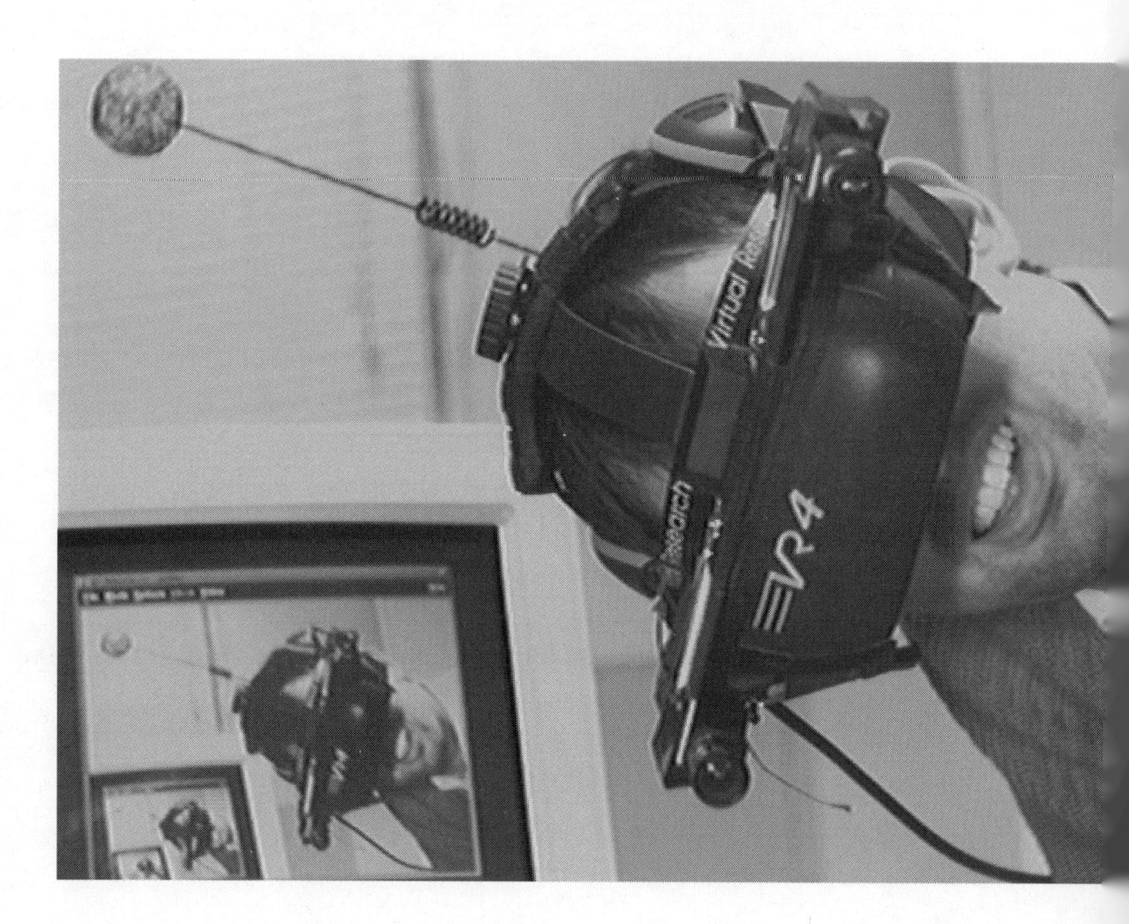

[virtual life]

Jennifer Ringley

can identify more with the fish who are being watched (as I mentioned before) than those doing the watching. That's because for the last year and a half she's suffered from a self-inflicted bout of 'Looking at the world through the Web' syndrome that has turned her life over to the public domain.

Jennifer, a twenty-something student, attached a digital video camera to her Internet-equipped computer and left it on 24 hours a day, capturing everything she did – study, cooking, many hours of sleeping – and undressing! What leads a person to such a life? In a newspaper column outlining her position earlier last year, Jennifer described it as a desire to bring into the open all the 'secret' moments of people's lives. 'Why don't we all decide to collectively get over it and have a good time being whoever we are, without embarrassment?' she wrote.

jennifer's site

Jennifer Ringley's site

http://www.jennicam.org

[virtual life]

But the problem is that Jennifer's experiment with public self-consciousness (or, as some others have commented to me 'self exhibitionism') turned into something slightly more. She was 'uncovered' by an Australian computer magazine through a series of letters, culminating in the publication of her website address. Immediately hundreds of people logged on, hoping to catch a glimpse of Ringley in a compromising position (reports have said she played for the cameras, often teasing the primarily male audience from around the world). Jennifer was forced to close down her site because of the huge Internet bills for the thousands of visitors accessing her site. While she directed her anger towards the magazine to begin with, she seems to be over that now – and has found the funds to continue the site, nude and all. 'Be a little bolder than the next link,' writes Ringley, 'I'll start.' ¶

melrose place in cyberspace?

SPOTNIK

When the soap was invented back then (some time in the past), I'm sure its inventor never thought that one day computer screens, not television, would be the media of choice. But that's the way it's going as soap operas move away from the linear 80s and 90s into the next interactive century.

Soap operas are one of a set of new uses that move the Internet away from being only a handy communication tool, into a fun entertainment medium.

The first Internet soap opera was a 'series' of stories called 'Parallel Lives' on the *New York Times* information service on America Online. Plot twists were suggested by readers. The idea was there, but not much else.

The Spot was the first Internet soap opera to have much success. In fact *The Spot* has had a **lot** of success. It began in June 1995 with the plot based around 5 young twenty-somethings (on my visit they were Tara, Lon, Carrie, Michelle, and Jeff) who all just happened to look like they'd stepped out of a fashion magazine (as in most soaps) and their dog, Spotnik (no relation to the Russian rocket).

Each day, the group would post a diary entry about what had happened in their lives – you know, love, parties, friends, etc. Here's one from my favourite character, the dog (did you know dogs could write?):

. . . She likes to walk very fast, which is fine with me. Sometimes, I have to pull on her leash when she gets too far ahead of me.

the spot

She seems to forget that there is a lot of territory that I need to re-mark and smell. Also, I don't think she notices all of the male humans that smile, sniff, and wink at her. I try to get her to stop and smile back, but she just pats me on the head and off we go. What can I say? . . . I do what I can. But, the best thing about taking her for a walk is that she always shares her snacks with me. I've tried to do the same thing, but she just smiles and returns it . . .

WHO'S who at the spot

According to Internet folklore, *The Spot* was left up to an advertising agency to produce. No one could work out how they could possibly make money from a website that obviously cost quite a bit to keep 'fresh' – but didn't go over the top with huge advertising slogans scrawled across every page. However, *The Spot* tried something different. These were not just any old ads – they actually wove them into the plot lines of the soap.

So whenever the characters went out for a romantic dinner there was always a big spiel in their journal the next day about how good the food was in a particular restaurant (that just happened to be paying *The Spot's* owners lots of money). This kind of advertising is used in most Internet soaps at the moment, because if it's used carefully it doesn't detract from the story.

Since *The Spot* was launched, many Internet soaps have sprung up – a lot are more technologically advanced. Most on-line soaps now have sound, music, and even video to add to the diary entries. Some even let you IRC (Internet Relay Chat) with the characters.

The computer is a different and new thing for the soap

opera. You feel much closer to the characters and much more 'at the scene'. We can check up on details that we simply couldn't know before, by reading the characters' diaries, for instance. We can find out their personal feelings towards each other in an interactive way. You can't just sit on the couch with your eyes glued to the telly – now your fingers have to be glued to the mouse as well.

The Spot **http://www.thespot.com**

Other soaps to try:

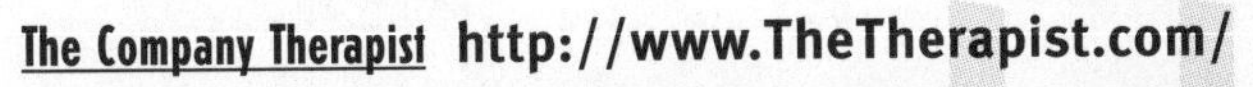

The Company Therapist **http://www.TheTherapist.com/**
There are a lot of weird people out there on the Net. So why not make a Net drama about them? That's the premise for Dr Charles Balis, the fictional lead of this site. 'Depression, schizophrenia, addiction, violence', basically sums up the plot. Help!

Cracks in the Web **http://www.directnet.com/~gmorris/title.html**
This is an espionage crime drama, out weekly on the Net.

The Squat **http://www.thesquat.com/welcome.html**
Sick of Spotnick and his tiresome owners?
Visit *The Squat!*

[FIDO the microchip]

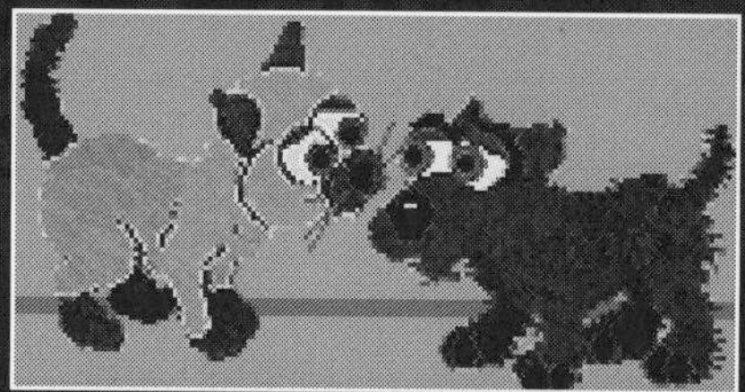

Virtual cameras are just one part of the 'looking at the world through the Web phenomenon.' Another is the virtual pet, made famous with the Tamagotchi by Japanese toy maker Bandai. You know – those little plastic watch-type things which children as old as 25 have dangling around their necks. They wake their 'parent' up at 6 in the morning with a loud 'BEEP' and demand to be fed (What do they eat? Bytes?) 4 times daily, put to bed with a kiss, and a myriad of other things. If you don't look after it properly it promptly says goodbye and dies. Unfortunately the record that any Tamagotchi has lived is about 35 days or something . . . so they don't last long. Perhaps that is because some devious person has asked for a look, and then surreptitiously pressed the reset button. Next time you're lucky to be around when this happens, watch the 'parent' and their look of anguish, and you might even feel a touch of sorrow.

On a happier note, Tamagotchi's immediately incur some sort of digital rebirth – surely giving joy to millions of Buddhists worldwide. In fact this raises another interesting question . . . Do Tamagotchi's come in both male and female varieties, or is the birth somewhat more mystical? Perhaps I'll leave that there.

If you're into the more traditional pets, but can't afford the food, then having some Dogz or Catz walking around on your computer screen may be the answer. In many ways the electronic animal alternatives combine the best parts of both the Tamagotchis and the real-life creature – and add a clever little screen-saver to an otherwise dull operating system. Now you even have the choice of turning it off if you're busy – a big design plus which the flesh-and-bone dogs and cats just can't match! ¶

VIRTUAL PETS

tamagotchi http://www.bandai.co.jp

dogz & catz http://www.dogz.com

or http://www.catz.com

lost IN space

Science Fiction – you either get it or you don't. Sometimes I feel like going back in time in H.G. Wells's time machine, to convince Jules Verne that being an accountant is a really cool job (oops, did I say cool?) and killing off the genre of SF before it could begin. But I must admit, late-night TV would be pretty boring without at least a couple of versions of Star Trek to choose from.

SCANNING FOR BEAM DOWN LOCATION

http://www.worldkids.net/jaguar
http://www.ufk.org

Speaking of Star Trek, Gregory Boubel is a webmaster 'boldly going where no kid has gone before'. In fact, we shouldn't call Greg a webmaster – admiral is a much more suitable word. Greg is the creator of USS Jaguar, the 'first, and largest Star Trek club for the younger fans on the Net'. The Jaguar, as Greg fondly calls it, is a ship (similar to the Enterprise) set up in all its HTML glory. It's a fascinating concept. As you move from deck to deck (or page to page) you can read the captain's log, and other stories about the adventures of the gallant crew, participate in various Star Trek games in live sessions, and talk about the latest episodes, among other activities.

Over the past year, Greg's site has grown to such a size that he had to split it up into a series of ships – and the United Federation of Kids was formed. UFK tries to provide a place for other fan clubs to join where they too can become ships in the Federation, all communicating with each other. 'It makes it more fun if you can see what they are doing,' says Greg.

It seems Greg's main regret is that Jaguar has not been endorsed as the 'official' kids Star Trek fan club. With an obviously large flow of people regularly visiting the site, Greg is able to compete with the more commercial ventures, but seems more relaxed about money. 'It is intended to help kids discover Star Trek . . . not for me to see dollar signs.'

While we're at this weird journey through the ether, have a look at some other great sites:

addresses

Sci-Fi Insults

http://members.aol.com/DMD7371067/insults.html

Insults and Science Fiction go hand in hand, so it's not surprising that someone has finally got around to collecting them all together (and putting them in alphabetical order, no less). At this site you'll find gems ranging from **Blithering Blatherskite** and **Doddering Dunderhead** to **Clumsy Cloot**! (Note, however, that this is an America Online site – unless AOL is your ISP you won't be able to access this.)

Boldly Go Where No Kid Has Gone Before!

The Slightly Warped Sliders Page

http://www.geocities.com/Area51/Dimension/2301/sliders.html

Run, run like hell! It's the slightly warped sliders page. Flying pancakes, planets full of zombies and the characters from 'South Park' cross paths with Mulder and Scully – watch out you don't end up on ER's operating table with Xena chopping away at your head in the pop culture ride of your life. Beam me up, Scotty! Quick!

Matt's Red Dwarf Page

http://members.harborcom.net/~kliotj/reddwarf/

Made by the show's self-proclaimed 'biggest fan', this site has plenty of stuff to keep you busy, like . . . reading the scripts to yourself? Well, I suppose that could be exciting . . .

Red Dwarf vs. Star Trek

http://www.afn.org/~afn34967/rdvvoy/rdvvoy.html

But if a WAR is more your style, jump over to the most evenly matched dogfight in all history (of the imaginary future, that is). The Red Dwarf is squaring off against the starship Voyager, and you wouldn't want to miss a minute of the action! And tune in for the next exciting episode where two holograms take drastic action . . .

Hercules and Xena

http://www.play.net/simunet_public/hx/hxhome.asp

This site gave me the chills . . . the ability to actually be Xena: Warrior Princess. That's right boys and girls, an on-line game.

'on air' on-line

It's the ABC, it's the Top 10 – no, it's RealAudio, the super new technology that streams sound to your computer faster than a speeding bullet!

You could be forgiven these days if you turned on your computer and thought that you must have switched on a radio somewhere. But no, all this sound is coming through your Internet connection. RealAudio is a revolutionary bit of software, which compresses sound files to make them much smaller, so they can 'stream' across your low-bandwidth Net connection.

I've explained before that the Net is the amateur publisher's dream because it lets anyone deliver thousands of copies of their latest documents to anyone who asks for them. With RealAudio, the Net is now the amateur radio announcer's dream too. Anyone (with a very small amount of money and an impressive list of technical skills) can broadcast songs, news and just about anything else they want.

So far, as with any new and exciting technology, the amateur broadcasters are just starting to move onto the Net. But it is the real-life radio stations, with relatively more resources, both large and small from right around the world, which have jumped on-line to go global.

If you can name a country, you can probably listen to a live (or at least delayed) broadcast direct from a local station, as well as the Top 40 hits and some entertainment shows – and the sound quality is remarkably good too! RealAudio is now one of the most popular (and impressive) things on-line.

You can find a list of lots of sites listed at the directory produced by RealAudio creators, Progressive Networks.

ABC (America) provides hourly news updates which can be downloaded, but going one better is the Fox News Network, which reproduces its cable television station live on the Web.

The International Relay network provides a really good service reproducing radio station news services from around the world, including very impressive services from Radio Australia and UN Radio. For computer industry news, try the bulletin produced by the technology supremos, CNET, which complements their television and Web-based coverage.

Apart from the sound, RealVideo is also starting to make its mark, although this is more limited by the slow speeds at which connection is possible today. (You have to have a sound card and speakers, obviously, to get any sound from the Internet!)

RealAudio and Video **http://www.real.com**
ABC News (US) **http://www.abcnet.net**
FOX News **http://www.foxnews.com**
Internet Relay Network **http://www.wrn.org**
CNET **http://www.cnet.com**

ANOTHER SITE FOR TV FANS . . .

The Official South Park Site
http://www.comedycentral.com/southpark/

@ ~~mr~~ showbiz!

The Internet really took off in about the middle of 1995. Before then there wasn't a whole lot of stuff for people to look at on the WWW – mainly just some government files and some teaching notes left from the time when the Internet was a government and, later, educational network. But that started to change, and one of the first people to create some interesting content was Roger Davidson. Where to begin? Roger, an avid film watcher and movie goer, decided to start writing his own reviews – and, with the help of his programmer-father, began the almost legendary 'Teen Movie Critic'. Roger's reviews were on any and every movie he watched – not necessarily just new ones, and his rating system was unusually opinionated.

teenage movie critic

the teenage movie critic
http://www.dreamagic.com/roger/teencritic.html

As you can probably imagine, The Teen Movie Critic, being one of the most interesting sites on an empty Web (let alone the fact that he was 15!), became extremely popular among Net surfers who regularly came in their droves to see his opinions. After USA Today called him an 'on-line celeb', Roger's site was picked by Netscape (maker of the popular Internet browsing software), as a

@ mr showbiz!

'Cool' site – and it remained on their list for over a year. This amount of attention gave his reviews an audience of 300,000 people EVERY day. Roger has also been in *People* magazine, the *New York Times* – and received letters from Bill Clinton!

So what does it feel like to be famous? Roger told me he feels a little different. 'Talking to millions of people all over the world can give you quite a rush', he wrote. I should think it would. Anyway, Roger believes that if other people want to write and publish on the Web like him then 'they should go for it', because the Net is the 'perfect place for your voice to be heard'. He believes that the Internet is a great tool, because it lets you communicate with people all over the world. 'Communication . . . is no more than a keyboard away!'

Of course, all good things must come to an end – and you can't really have a Teenage Movie Critic who isn't a teen. After 2 years of working away at the site, as part of his home schooling, Roger has posted his last review. But the site will remain as a landmark, in the history of the World Wide Web. ¶

the teenage movie critic http://www.dreamagic.com/vivian/teencritic.html

Vivian Rose, new Teen Movie Critic

the truth

chapter 5

i§ out there

kooks & spooks
just plain weird

weird@Web

From kooks and spooks to just plain weird, the Net is the place for the **paranormal, strange** and **morbid** information on the world around us and the people that inhabit it (or used to at least . . .). **Conspiracies that leave no stone unturned** and every angle qualified cover the Web. **Aliens** on the attack use it for communication – and **celebrities** are hidden, lurking to escape their star-struck lives.

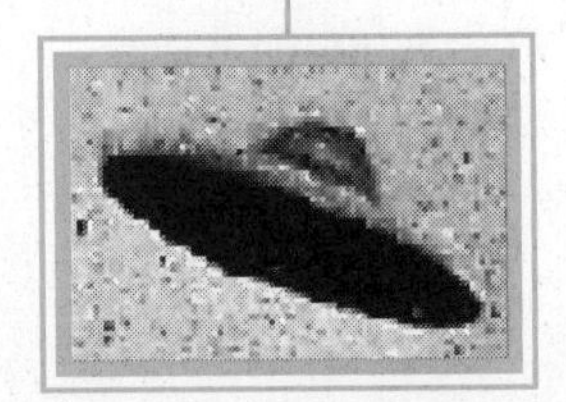

not dead on the Web!

Although Elvis has been dead for quite some time (sorry, but it's a fact) the people of the Internet have not forgotten him. In fact the Internet is now home to many of the world's most fanatical Elvis groups!

You might not think that the 'King' is really that closely related to religion – but after a quick trip around the on-line world you will soon see otherwise. The Internet is full of every kind of group, church, sect, order, and cult – a weird mixture of beliefs and ideas. These are not just your normal churches, where you might go for a quiet Sunday's prayer.

Just like other religious styles, the Elvis followers are in the business of 'spreading the word'. The 24 Hour Church of Elvis – Unofficial Website even has articles written by believers explaining when they were converted:

> Driving down Burnside in west downtown Portland I saw a little unassuming yet colorful sign at the corner of 8th Avenue. Driving too fast to read the words, I did manage to make out the word 'Elvis'. I immediately made the turn down 8th, as if some strange force was guiding me (I was later to find out this strange force was probably the King himself). I shortly found myself at 720 SW Ankeny, in front of a bland grey two storey store front that gave no hint of the enlightenment to be found within. Another small decorative sign pointed at the entrance to the staircase leading up to . . . the 24 Hour Church of Elvis! My upper lip began to twitch . . . my leg started shaking rhythmically . . . I knew I was very close.

According to the 24 Hour Church's own description it is –

a Church that operates like a bank machine. It is part of Where's the Art!!, the World's First 24 Hour Coin-Operated Art Gallery, located for the last seven years in Portland, Oregon. The Church of Elvis offers a wide variety of services, all priced moderately from one to four quarters, including weddings, confessions, catechisms, sermons, and photo opportunities with the King. Legal weddings are also available for $25 and up.

The Elvis following on the Web is really amazing. There are ***hundreds*** of websites that include pictures, sound, articles and letters from readers. Many people also claim to have seen Elvis walking down their local street.

However, that Elvis is still alive is not something that the creators of the next Elvis site believe. They haven't started up a new faith based around the words to his songs. All they claim is that they have a para-normal experience where they talked to Elvis via a seance – pretty normal people really! They've kindly given us an interpretation of his answers to help those not so connected with the dead:

QUESTION:* *Elvis, are you in this room?
ANSWER:* *Yes

INTERPRETATION:* *We were overjoyed to find out that our efforts had indeed summoned the King. From this answer we can also postulate that Elvis must then be dead. (Reincarnation was out of the question as all persons present were older than 17 years). However, he could have been alive, but outside of our view, i.e. looking in through our window.

Some webmasters have decided that they like the idea of founding a faith. The Eighth Day Transfigurist Cult is one of these sites:

That's it for now, but the final version will include a more detailed description of our vision of the King in 1989, and instructions for the rituals.

See, even religions suffer from the 'Under Construction' syndrome. It's probably lucky that Elvis is dead – imagine what the following would be like if he wasn't.

addresses

The 24 Hour Church of Elvis Official Website **http://www.churchofelvis.com**
8th Day Transfigurist Cult **http://sunsite.unc.edu/elvis/cult.html**
An Elvis Seance **http://sunsite.unc.edu/elvis/seance.html**

Some other sites to try:

Who killed Elvis? **http://www.on.net/users/rob/psychic/elvis.html**
A serious psychic report on the role of the zodiac in Elvis's death.

The Doghaus Elvis Collection **http://www.doghaus.com/**
An Elvis collectable on-line gallery. If you want 'The King Lights Up My Life – Elvis Matches', an Elvis Cookbook or a cool Elvis Licence Plate, then guess what? You've come to the right place.

conspiracy theories and alien invaders

Conspiracy Theories and UFOs are the kinds of things that don't get much attention on the serious media – mainly in dramas like ***The X-Files***. This is because the people that run these set-ups usually don't believe in them. Now if you had people who claimed they had been abducted by aliens as executives in every television station and newspaper in the country, a lot more weird and unexplained ideas would surface.

This was the way it was until someone invented the Net. The Net is the amateur publisher's dream and it lets anyone put up their weird crackpot ideas all over the wired world.

The World Wide Web plays host to so many **cover-ups** and **public subversion activities** that after reading for a while you begin to believe that ***everything*** that happened in the last 50 years has just been **one big plot**.

The Conspiracies site is a great start. Did you know Russia has an operating Star Wars system, that Humankind never actually landed on the moon and that AIDS was invented by the CIA for use in wars!?!

Thankfully not everyone on the Internet believes that the earth being round was a conspiracy started by some man with a telescope. One thing you can always trust on the Web is that someone is out there having a laugh at what someone else thinks and kindly creating a satire. The Department of Conspiracy Investigation and Propagation was, according to its website:

> created by President Nixon to fill a much needed void. Previously, conspiracies in America were a haphazard, slipshod, and unregulated affair. With the creation of the DCIP, America leapt ahead of international competitors in the conspiracy field. The department charter is to 'investigate unknown, and therefore unregulated, conspiracies to ensure minimum duplication of effort and maximum efficiency; to obfuscate and derail foreign investigation of domestic conspiracies; and to promote the creation, funding, and perpetuation of existing domestic conspiracies'.

The official-looking site lets you read about 'current cases it's working on', and even fill out a form to submit your own details of plots you have uncovered to take over the world.

Currently the big conspiracy theory going round on the Internet concerns the comet Hale Bopp, which passed over our skies in March 1997. The Hale Bopp Conspiracy Page is a very detailed site at the hub of all the interest. It was in fact where the discussion started when an investigator and amateur astronomer posted some odd pictures of the comet. Now, the site hosts so many conspiracies that I'm starting to believe them. A lot of coincidences together make a pretty believable argument. Everyone from NASA to the CIA to the Vatican seems to be involved in the plot. They include such ideas as Buzz Aldren holding a strange and mystical offering to Orion after landing on the moon where he 'consumed wine', and that aliens will soon be here in hordes (although that idea has been around for some time).

addresses

Conspiry http://wiretap.area.com/Gopher/Library/Fringe/Conspiry/

The Department of Conspiracy http://www.conspiracy.org

Other sites you may like to look at:

50 Greatest Conspiracies of all Time http://www.conspire.com

Web e-zine and book dedicated to the study of the paranormal and political cover-ups.

Alt.alien.visitors

The special newsgroup where aliens can 'phone home'!

International Society for UFO Research http://www.isur.com

As the name suggests, everything you need to know about unidentified flying objects.

big brother on the Web . . .

The Bavarian Illuminati Website is reputed to be the official homepage of the group that claims to have controlled the world for over 100 years without anyone else noticing. They have plans to fix just about any problem in the world and here's a snippet of one aimed at 'rescuing the dollar':

```
The US dollar's continued slide against
international currencies has come at an
inopportune time for the Illuminati.
Luckily, market forces can correct the problem.
You can help the Illuminati by burning every
last piece of US currency available to you. This will decrease the
supply of dollars, and, in turn, drive up their value. If you have large
quantities of cash and do not have the time for the hassle of burning
it, send email with the subject 'take money' and we will make
arrangements to pick it up.
```

THE B FILES

Looking to see what else I could find on this up until now elusive group, I stumbled across a number of anti-Illuminati groups (obviously some disillusioned ex-supporters) including the CIA (or rather, the 'Counter Illuminati Agency') who have taken it upon themselves to expose the Bavarian baddies.

```
The CIA is dedicated to unravelling . . . and recording the conspiracy
that is world domination. Who are the Illuminati? They are the power
behind the power. They are THE secret society (shush, it's a secret).
```

ACCESS DENIED

In one slightly sadistic press release they claim Princess Diana was murdered 'by those who schemed to do the princess in, to further their own political agenda (you know who)'.

However, rather unfortunately they '. . . at the Counter-Illuminati Agency will only pass along those facts which we can verify . . . [and we] can't affirm to the dependency [of our informants]', so they couldn't go into any more details. They do however promise that they usually use the most reliable sources.

For those conspiracy junkies in the Texas area, you can even join a service provider called Illuminati Online. From what we could gather, they are not officially a branch of the secret society, but the world power brokers must get their email access from somewhere . . .

Counter Illuminati Agency **http://www.merlins-cave.com/cia/**
Illuminati Online **http://www.io.com**

And see opposite for . . .

addresses

The X-MAS Files
http://christmas.com/xmas.files/xmas.files.html

WHO SAID **SANTA** DOESN'T EXIST?

It all started when a mysterious email entered my in-box: 'NEWS FLASH: Investigators have found proof that Santa Claus exists!'

What person could possibly pass up such an intriguing invitation to read more? (Yes, yes, a sane one, you say.) So I delved into the mystery . . .

Christmas.com looks like yet another terribly boring company trying to milk a few more dollars out of the same old Santa theme to 6-year-olds who don't know any better. But delve a little deeper, and you'll find one of the Web's gems – THE X-MAS Files . . .

Children and adults alike commonly come to the conclusion that there is no Santa Claus. To disprove this myth, our team was assembled – the best researchers, investigators, photographers and cameramen in the world. These are the findings of OUR mission, Project X-MAS.

When President Clinton was notified later that he indeed spoke with Saint Nick, he was quoted as saying, 'I thought the Jolly Old Guy knew way too much about whether I've been naughty or nice'.

There is a detailed fact-file and some slightly dubious (but very funny) photos.

Another great idea, though not yet fully realised, is SledEx – a 'not-too-serious parody of the overnight delivery company that Santa turns to when presents absolutely have to be under the tree by Christmas morning?' I never really believed he could fit them all in the sleigh anyway.

However, Susan Shinkai (a self-titled 'revisionist and idealist') thinks differently. She has come up with what seems to be certainly one of the most important discoveries of this century – that of 'Christmas Physics'.

Christmas Physics is a distant cousin of quantum theory. The Christmas phenomenon energy units, or 'Santas', are convertible to units of standard energy, time and space. This allows for the apparent impossibilities of flying reindeer, around-the-world trips in one night, etc.

Oh yeah, and while you're at it, the alt.religion.santaism newsgroup is a must visit for would-be elves.

celebrities, gossip and did Kurt Cobain really kill himself?

The Internet as a form of media doesn't have many of its own celebrities. It's a bit early in its life. That's probably why Internet surfers seem to like stars from the other media so much. Television personalities and Hollywood icons are almost sure to have a dozen or so pages dedicated to their worship. Fan clubs, picture pages, sound clips and biographies have all found their way onto the World Wide Web. Usenet, always one of the more trivial areas, has a huge library of groups interested in the celebs. It's a bit funny then, with all this star following, that many celebrities who find the real world a harder place to be in since they got all those fans, are now heavily into the Web as a way of escaping them. They like to hover, lurking around newsgroups about themselves, reading the articles posted by others anonymously, and sometimes reply when they think someone got it wrong. Sandra Bullock (who actually starred in the movie *The Net* a few years back) is known as a bit of a 'lurker'.

The Internet is a 'high-speed method of communication for the movement of information over long distances' **(as the dictionary**

would say) – the **perfect medium** for the **spreading of gossip.**

What REALLY happened to
Kurt Cobain?
click here
to find out!

When Kurt Cobain supposedly committed suicide a rumour went around the Web. Was he murdered? Although the same bit of gossip did the rounds in the newsstands, the loyal Nirvana fans were instantly alert on the Net. The arguments and counter arguments circulated around the newsgroups, websites were set up (Tom Grant's was one of the first) with semi-official reports, opinions and fact after fact and rumour after rumour. The Internet was now the Judge, Jury, Witness and Coroner – and it was trying to reach its verdict.

Courtney Love and Michael Dewitt, the male nanny living at the Cobain residence, were involved in a conspiracy that resulted in the murder of Kurt Cobain. It appears this was not the first attempt on Cobain's life by Courtney Love. It was, however, the first to succeed.

click here
to find out!

from Tom Grant's murder investigation site:

click here to find out!

first there was the motive:

Motivated by profit over truth as well as a web of business deals and personal career considerations, Courtney Love, her attorneys, and many of Courtney's industry supporters have engaged in an effort to keep the public from learning the real facts of this case.

the witness:

Courtney knew Kurt wanted out of the marriage. Just weeks prior to his death, she asked one of her attorneys to get the 'meanest, most vicious divorce lawyer' she could find.

the evidence:

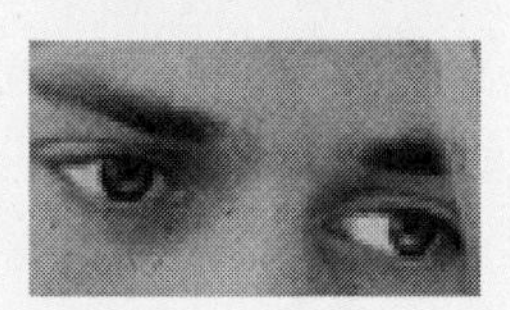

One of Kurt's credit cards was missing when his body was discovered. Someone was attempting to use the missing credit card after Cobain died, but the attempts stopped when his body was discovered.

and finally, the verdict:

The police and the Medical Examiner have no forensic evidence that proves Cobain's death was a suicide. On the other hand, there's a substantial amount of evidence for murder. The official verdict of 'suicide' was simply a rush to judgement which eventually painted the authorities into a corner as reports of so-called 'copy-cat' suicides began making the news.

and here's the press release:

Although they've managed to hamper and slow the process, letters to my office from all over the world indicate Courtney's attempts to censor the truth are not working!

<u>The Kurt Cobain Murder Investigation Site</u>
http://www.musica.org/nirvana/murder/murder.html

<u>D.P's Nirvana Page</u> **http://www.netcom.com/~dperle/nirvana/index.html**
A great source of information featuring Nirvana, but special mention must go to the very detailed account of why Tom Grant's 'Murder Investigation Site' mentioned above is false: if you consider yourself a rationally-thinking human being, and if you have been sucked into Tom Grant's world, this document should almost definitely make you rethink being so quick to believe in the investigation.

Well, in every murder case there are conflicting tales . . .

write to the stars!

Many celebs hang out on-line – why not send them a message? Many people have put up sites listing famous people's email addresses. Here are a few of the better ones I have found, but you can always go and search for others that might interest you too.

Madonna	madonna@wbr.com
Bill Gates	bgates@microsoft.com
President Clinton	president@whitehouse.gov
Chelsea Clinton	chelsea@whitehouse.gov
Beavis	beavis@mtv.com
Butthead	butthead@mtv.com
Dalai Lama	tere@unv.ernet.in
Ronald McDonald	ronald@mcdonalds.com.com
Santa	Santa@north.pole.org
Sandra Bullock	sandra6226@aol.com
Scott Adams	scottadams@aol.com

becoming

chapter six
a Netizen

a quick guide to Netiquette

Just like in the real world, you have to be nice to people on the Internet. But as the Internet isn't the real world – it's a weird collection of bits and bytes spewing out of computers around the world, as I explained earlier – a new code of conduct had to be invented. Exactly who this responsibility fell on, I'm not quite sure, but they certainly did a very thorough job – and came up with **Netiquette . . .**

No New Mail
Sorry, you don't have any new mail
because you're a dork.
OK

The behavioural code called Netiquette was designed with mainly email and newsgroups in mind, but recently a whole new set of rules relating to the World Wide Web has started to appear, although this is mainly to do with Web page design (and that can be found later in Chapter 8). Believe me, it's right back to learning to eat with a knife and fork all over again.

EMAIL ETIQUETTE

your signature

SIGNATURES

Signatures are very handy little bits of text that you can write once, and automatically attach to every single email file you send – sort of like an electronic business card. NEVER make your signature more than 8 lines long. NEVER include any type of text art (letters arranged to look like a picture). It is really, really annoying to see some huge picture of something that is meant to be your cat, or dog, you, or whatever – I wish text art had never been invented. It does not look good!!!!!!

Also, do not include quotes or cute symbols. These are really

B-O-R-I-N-G!

Some people look really silly including a RL address and phone number in their signatures. Who replies to emails by post?

(Well, not often anyway . . .) And it's probably not a good idea to put all your details down anyway, just for added security reasons.

SPELLING

Although you may think it's cool to write a nice long email and spell every single word incorrectly, I don't – and neither does anyone else. The best thing is to check, and then check again. Many email programs now come with in-built spell checkers. If yours doesn't and you have trouble working out whether **i** goes before or after **e**, then why not type your letter in a word processor file and then cut and paste into the email program? This one applies to USENET as well.

HOW TO PICK A SUBJECT

Keep it short, clear and precise and don't include too many **ands**. The subject is meant to help people decide which stuff is urgent and which isn't, so help them and feel a better person for it.

NEWSGROUP ETIQUETTE

CHOOSING A GROUP

NEVER decide that just because you can send your email to 100 or so newsgroups, you should. This is one of the worst rules to break, but it is one of the more common mistakes. Some people seem to think that the Net exists to give them an audience – it doesn't. Try and be really specific about the groups that you choose. If you are posting a follow-up to a message that was sent to more than one group try and send your message to only the groups related to the specific things you have mentioned.

HOW TO CHOOSE A SUBJECT

When choosing a subject for your messages, be specific – do not try and grab a wider audience by including a message that is short and meaningless. Remember the word 'subject' means **what something is about** – not just a catchy phrase to lure unknowing fools to read your message.

TONE IS IMPORTANT

When writing a message to a newsgroup (or even just someone via email), always try and be nice if you can. DO NOT start insulting other people or say anything outrageous, if that's possible. Sarcasm doesn't always work printed on the Net because the meanings can come across slightly skewed. If you really have to say something sarcastic, make sure the readers know exactly what you are saying by adding emoticons (see later in this chapter):

A: :)

OR EVEN: 'THAT'S NOT MEANT TO BE FUNNY'

(if you think that isn't too daggy).

OTHER IMPORTANT THINGS TO REMEMBER

When writing a message make sure the text wraps inside an area that will suit most users. People hate having to scroll backwards and forwards reading lines and lines of however interesting writing. Most of them will probably move on to something else. Try not to send too many attachments. These are other files or programs you can send with your email. If people have to download a large file to view your message, then they probably won't be bothered reading it.

what happens if you have bad manners

The citizens of the Net are notorious for their good Netiquette and believe me, they are very quick to frown upon those they deem to have been bad.

Expect to get flamed – a Net word for the many hate letters you will receive in response to your lapse in manners. If this does happen, there is nothing you can really do about it except wait for it to stop or change email accounts.

If you want to do something naughty on purpose it's probably better to use one of the many anonymous mailing services popping up around the place. Even then, the technical side of Net users may come out and they will probably still find out a way to track you down. I'm not trying to encourage you here – just warn you.

a note on Net style

Communicating with the Internet is usually via written text. (Unless you're one of those with-it executive types who drive Porsches: they always use video conferencing or an Internet voice phone.)

On the Net you write just like you would talk. As most people can't type as fast as they can speak (although many would like to say they do), Netters use a lot of symbols, abbreviations and acronyms as a quick way to get around the speed problem. Punctuation is hardly ever used. As with email Netiquette, the Internet has its own rules that come into effect. To add importance and emphasis to what you're saying, use ***asterisks*** around the words or **JUST TYPE IN CAPITAL LETTERS**. And before we really get into it, remember the advice I gave you in the introduction. Do not overuse these words or techniques to show that you are a seriously wired dude. They're handy for conversation, nothing else. And now, here's a list of abbreviations and acronyms used all over the Net:

- **BRB** Be right back.
- **BTW** By the way.
- **FTF** Face to face (when you're actually talking to someone in real life - see RL).
- **IMHO** In my humble opinion - used to mean the exact opposite - usually WHEN YOU'RE USING CAPS LOCK!).
- **LOL** Laughing out loud (if you find something particularly funny, you might want to use this).
- **MOTD** Message of the Day.
- **POV** Point of view (what you think).
- **RL** Real Life (meaning when you're not connected to the Net - although for some the Net is their 'real life' and RL is just the time when you have to go to the door to pay the pizza man).
- **WYSIWYG** What you see is what you get.
- **YABA** Yet another bloody acronym!

girl power!

Okay, okay, this organisation isn't for everyone. It's not for me, but I have been told there are many girls out there (ahem!). **Girls Internationally Writing Letters** (see – G.I.R.L) was created in early 1996 by Monica Bough. She thought girls needed a place to hang out, and perhaps challenge the stereotype 'that only boys are interested in computers'. Unfortunately when I wanted to find out more, I came across one barrier which I hadn't thought about. I wasn't allowed inside (oops!). So I had to contact someone and find out exactly what they do in this exclusive, sexist organisation :-). Monica was away, so instead I got to talk to the acting President Gina, who explained that anyone can visit, but they do have a members only area for the girls. 'It's more a safety issue than a secret', she said.

So what goes on behind these closed doors? I was intrigued. 'We write letters to each other and try to help each

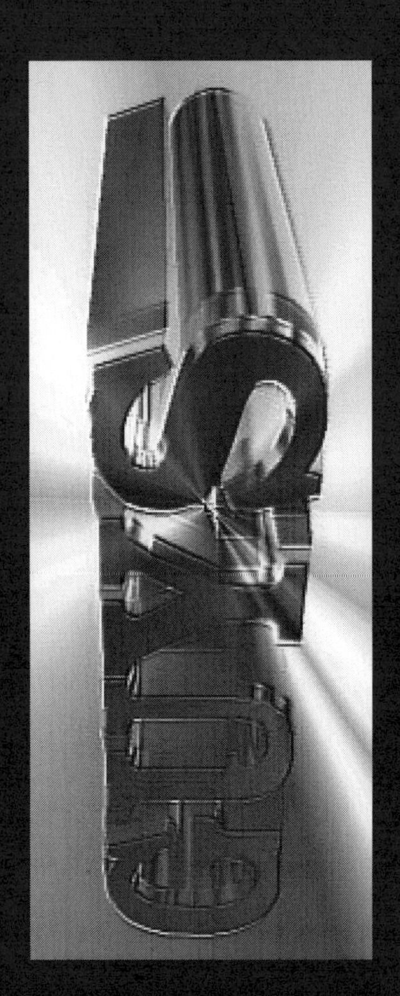

other out. We do a lot of activities, we sponsor the WKN (World Kids Network) Care Quest project – writing letters to kids in hospitals. We are just about making friends and having fun – and maybe doing something good in the meantime', she said. Ah, so that's it . . .

GIRL has been criticised a lot lately for being discriminatory. Gina just shrugs this off, and says, 'I am not a boy. As a matter of fact I am nothing like a boy and I LIKE it that way. I like boys the way they are and girls the way they are too. I have nothing against either – I am for both. We are equal, yet different. Friendship is the act of accepting our differences, and that teaches us to cherish our similarities.' Well, that's a point. Gina seems to think that equality is not compromised as long as there are clubs for Guys. There are.

GUYS is the club that has grown in response to GIRL. They do a lot of similar sorts of activities, and sometimes work together on various projects. GIRL and GUYS (and for that matter my own club TCN) are part of the sprawling World Kids Network website. WKN is a non-profit organisation which is dedicated to helping kids and teens learn more about the Internet – through donating Internet services to kid and teen-run organisations like GIRL.

Many companies are pouring $$ into trying to mimic the GIRL success, building flashy sites on a grand scale such as GirlTech. But GIRL is still going well – mainly because it is built and maintained by the girls themselves.Gina thinks one of GIRL's biggest achievements is helping to beat the old stereotypes. 'I think we have proved them wrong, especially the part about girls [and computers]. Girls love the Internet. It gives us a way to communicate.' ¶

addresses

<u>GIRL</u> **http://www.worldkids.net/girl/**
<u>GUYS</u> **http://www.worldkids.net/clubs/guys/**
<u>WKN</u> **http://www.worldkids.net/** <u>and</u> **http://www.wkn.org**
<u>Girl Tech</u> **http://www.girltech.com**

How do you get a smile out of :-) ???

emoticons

Emoticons are text symbols that can be used over the Net as a way of showing how you feel. It's a bit hard for others to tell sometimes when they can't hear your voice or see your body movements. Hundreds of these emoticons – more commonly called smileys – are around:

:-) The most **basic smiley**.
You are either **happy** or **sarcastic.**

:-(Something is **wrong**.
You are either **unhappy** or **depressed.**

:-> You're **so happy** that your mouth is somewhere up near your ears.

<:-(**Anger**.
WOULD YOU LIKE TO REPEAT THAT!!! <:-(

8–0 You are **shocked!**

:) Only **slightly funny** (or you are pretending to laugh at someone's pathetic joke).

:-0 **Yawn**. (How boring can you get?)

;-) The '**wink**' is also used fairly frequently!

face to face – chatting on the Net

Imagine 10 people in a room together. Now imagine that these 10 people have never met each other before. Now imagine that the 10 people are all talking to each other about different things. Now try and imagine what these people are saying to each other. Now imagine that sometimes a person comes and whispers something in your ear. And that these 10 people are actually on the other side of the world in a virtual room connected via the Internet. If you could do all that you would now have a pretty good idea of what IRC is. Hopefully by the time you have finished reading this little chapter you won't just have to imagine any more.

Internet Relay Chat is one of the many communication tools that can be used over the Internet and is separate to the World Wide Web and email. It lets you 'chat' by typing in messages to other users. Your message is displayed on the screen immediately for everyone else who's connected to see. That is, unless you have sent it privately to only one user.

The kind of conversations people have are very different to those in other Internet tools where messages can be sent, such as USENET. This is mainly because you are actually in a **live** conversation with the other participants, instead of sending your entire message and then waiting for a letter in response.

IRC is the most informal aspect of the Net and I think it is one of the most fun. One of the interesting things about IRC is that people usually don't use their real names, preferring to choose a nickname instead. This may seem a bit scary to a new user, but at least under a false identity people

hi there. my name is knuckle-duster. i like to read comics.

hiya. my name is python.

seem to be able to offer a much more interesting conversation, and can open up. It doesn't seem to matter that what they are saying is probably a fantasy. You're talking, and that is all that matters.

The first thing someone will usually say to you when you join a chat 'room' or channel is 'How old are you?' Because they can't see you they want to know what kind of person you are, so they know what kind of things they should say to you. Other basic questions such as 'What do you look like?' and 'Where do you live?' are also common. Another thing that's often asked (if your nickname doesn't give it away) is your sex – in other words, they want to know if they can go out with you sometime! People on IRC sometimes ask rather personal questions so be prepared! It's the kind of thing that you'll either love or hate.

A quick hint – if you're looking to have a decent quality conversation with anybody, IRC is probably not your easiest option, although if you go for the really specific chat rooms, you may find someone interesting to talk to. An example of these are the ones organised to supplement a television show or book launch. These usually have people there specially to guide the conversation and make sure it doesn't get off the topic. But whoever said that you were looking for a quality conversation?

IRC is usually run through a separate program such as MIRC on your computer although now there are also Web chats and Java chats.

Sites such as Talk.com (which is operated by the magazine *Wired*) often has celebrity guests appearing on its chat rooms at certain times, so keep a look out for them.

Probably one of the most popular chat areas on the Internet is Yahoo! Chat. There are normally over 250 people using it, so there is always someone to talk to.

To find out about chat groups probably the best place to start is the Yahoo Net Events! directory which has listings in the thousands. There **are** literally thousands of IRC channels, but one of the best places to start is Dalnet at http://www.dal.net. Dalnet is a chat server – and you can even make your own chat channels and rooms.

addresses

Talk.com **http://www.talk.com**
Yahoo! Chat **http://chat.yahoo.com**
Yahoo Net Events! **http://events.yahoo.com**
MIRC **http://www.mirc.com**

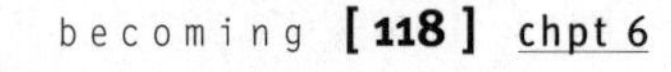

the **kayotic one!**

Ever journeyed out into the Abyss? Perhaps you should . . . The Kayotic Abyss is a collection of thoughts and observations of one 16-year-old about life, technology and the future. A rambling diary of scenarios, quotes and events, the Abyss is one of the most thought-provoking websites I've ever come across. Kayotic's entries range from rhetorical questions (there are a lot of these) on Software piracy:

> I read an article in Wired that said that in Asia, software pirates are selling Microsoft Office for $13, Myst for around $9, and AutoCAD Release 13 for about $6. Anyone have plane tickets to Asia?

and voice mail:

> What would it be like if you were the lady that says all the pre-recorded messages from the phone company? When you dialled a wrong number, wouldn't it be weird to hear you tell yourself that the number you dialled was no longer in use?

to some very true but perhaps controversial observations about us all:

> It is amazing how many kids on the Internet act completely stupid. They ask each other dumb questions (yes, there is such a thing as a dumb question) and they chat. I wonder what

percentage of the Web's resources are devoted to on-line chatting. The Web is slow and clunky: take away most of the chat systems, and the thing might run a little faster.

Kayotic's Journal is very nicely presented too, and also includes an art gallery for computer generated work, an area for discussion of his text, and (slightly amusingly) a Web chat room. :-) Kayotic's also an enthusiastic tennis player, and was participating in the US Nationals when I visited for my third or fourth time.

Prediction: By January 1998, the common person will prioritise checking his email just as high as going to the mailbox each day.

This future teller seems likely to be the next Nicholas Negroponte (back page guru for *Wired* magazine) . . . About the email, well, I do that already . . .

'Tell me, have you ever seen anything like this?' – Brad Pitt
'No . . .' – Morgan Freeman

A conversation in the movie Seven, about the Kayotic Journal.

addresses

The Kayotic Abyss http://www.cyberteens.com/abyss/
WIRED http://www.wired.com/wired/

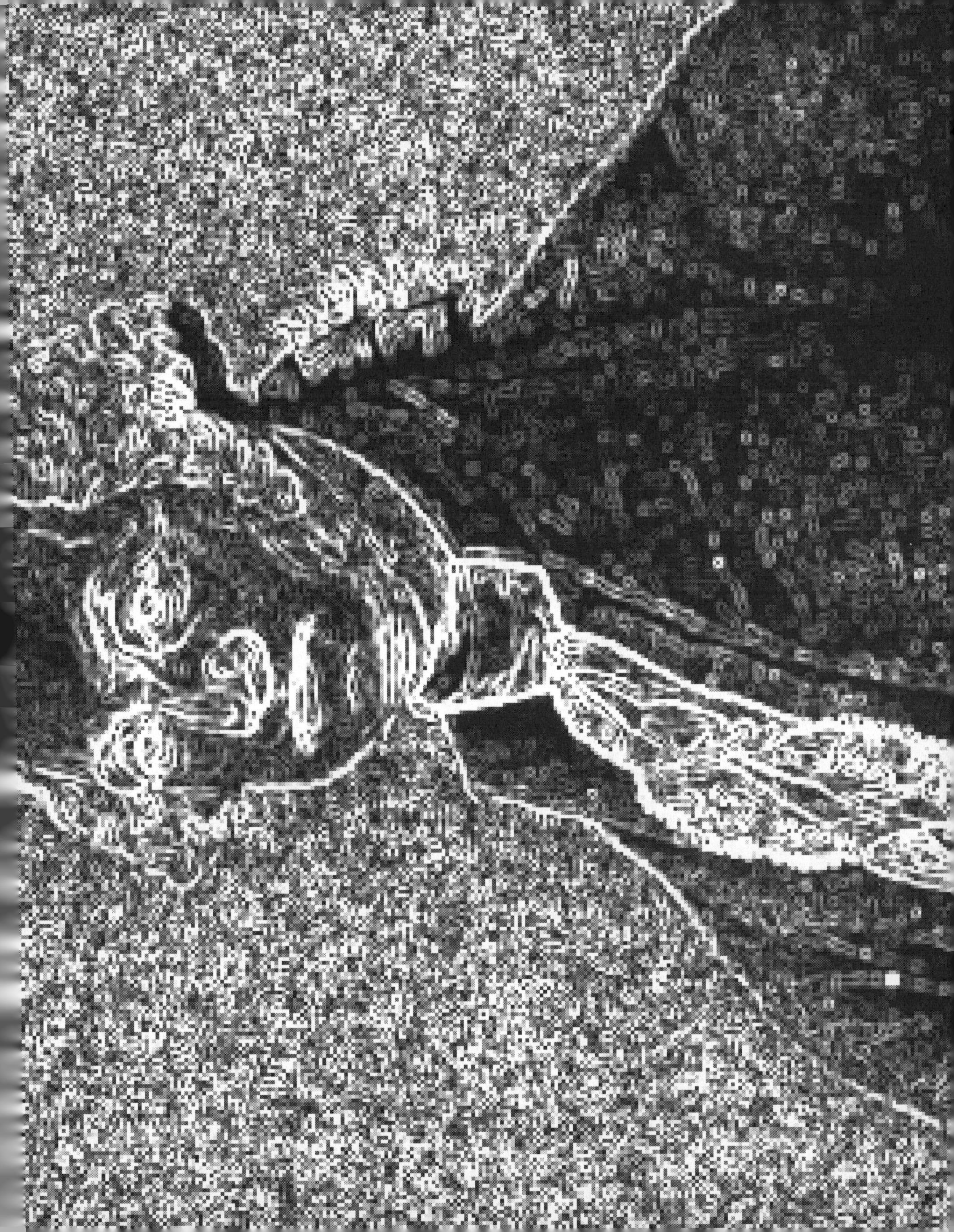

life's all

chapter 7
fun and games

fun & games in cyberspace

Games, Games, Games.

Why do people like playing games? It might surprise you that it's not because they are fun (well, it might be . . .). It's because people love being someone else – or at least being able to do something they couldn't do before.

The Internet is a bit like that too. People like the Internet primarily because of the gimmick – because it's something new – something they couldn't do before. They can be anonymous; they can even create a new identity. I once heard of a chat regular who had over 100 completely different personalities.

So it's not really surprising that chat and games have been linked. There are actually 2 types of on-line games, but they are both fun because they use the same principle. People like being someone (or something) else, and people like being someone else even more if others can see them being that someone. I know that sounds like complete nonsense on the first read, but try reading it again until you see the meaning – I'm sure it is there.

MUDs (people can't decide if this stands for Multi-User-Dungeons or Multi-User-Dimensions, even though it is over 8 years since they were invented). These are slightly obscure now, but still have a large following. Have you ever played any of those old text-based adventure games? The ones where you say 'Go right' or 'Look', and a nasty big monster comes and bites your head off? If you have, then it's really just a matter of thinking of them, and then thinking that the monster is a real person, so you can talk to them, in a similar way to Internet Relay Chat. And if you haven't, then I suggest you go down to your local software graveyard and pick up a copy of one.

As MUDs have evolved, the focus is now on your interactions and the virtual world that you travel around in. This is cyberspace left up to your imagination. There are whole communities and worlds to visit that are sometimes so big that you can lose yourself in them. Following on with the theme, the person who creates a MUD (usually through some kind of computer programming) is called a 'God'. They create the ‘virtual universe’. Some MUDs are so advanced that you can even add your own private neighbourhood to the cyberworld. There are fantasy MUDs, futuristic MUDs, even Star Trek MUDs (ever wanted to be Captain Kirk?).

MUDs let you create your own personality which remains part of the program even when you leave (your character just

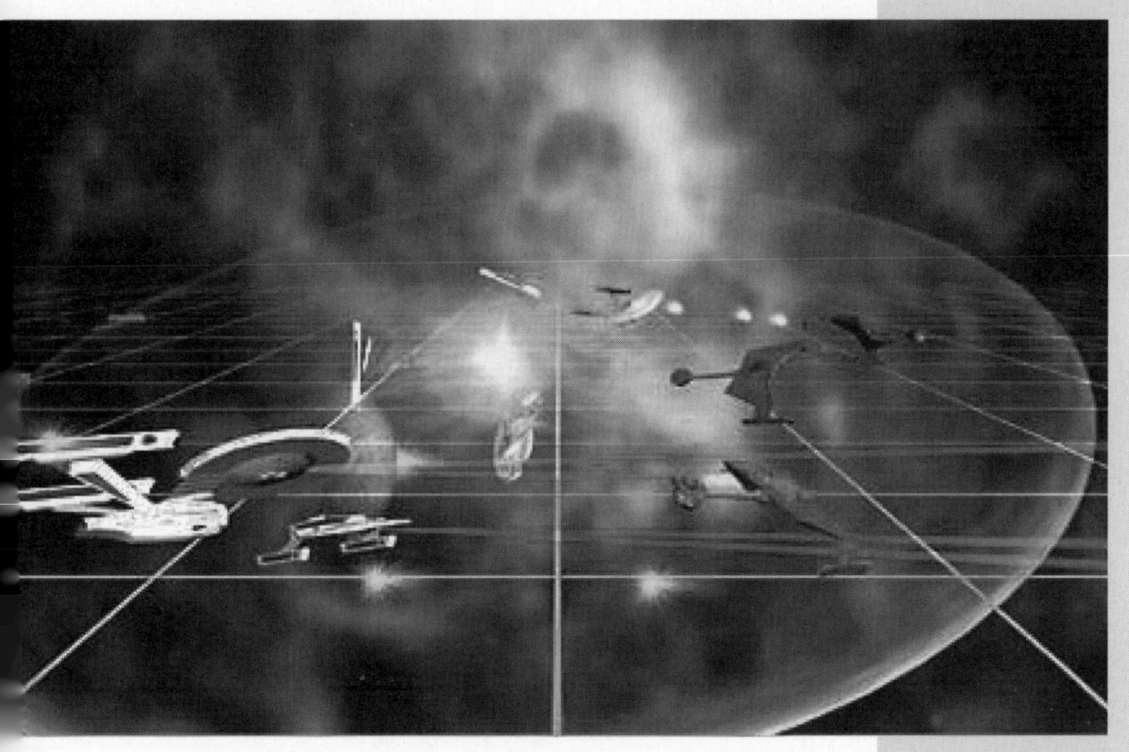

went to sleep). MUDs are really amazing places, and if you want a change from chat, try a MUD.

The other type of gaming on the Net is the simple network game. This is just your normal game that you play off your CD-ROM. This means that you can now have the experience of blowing up an alien or even try a bit of empire building with 30 (or more or less) people from right around the globe. Personally, I don’t find this much of a thrill, but I’m not that into games without a lot of social interaction.

People I know, however, spend weekends on the computer remotely competing in game battles on the Internet.

Some games are specially designed to be run over the Internet, but many others need some extra software that tricks the program into thinking it is being played over a Local Area Network (usually only a small number of computers connected together) rather than the much larger Internet. This software is called Kali and can be freely downloaded from lots of places on-line.

To play with other people you need to connect to a Kali Server. Many Internet Service Providers have special accounts for gamers that give them access to Kali Servers.

There are also many other types of small games on-line including Web-based Java games, if you want to explore these as well.

As well as being a great tool to play games over, the Internet has a huge collection of games-related information. Many commercial sites such as the Games Domain, Games Spot and Hyperactive have been set up specifically to provide games information.

If you think you won't play as many games once you are on the Net, you're wrong. You'll just spend more time on the computer!

addresses

Kali **http://www.kali.com**
Games Domain **http://www.gamesdomain.com**
Games Spot **http://www.gamespot.com**
Hyperactive **http://www.hyperactive.com**

When I joined up to the Internet, I got a book out of the library that I thought might give me a little introduction on how to use it. **Surfing on the Internet: A Nethead's Guide** was the one I picked up – and I couldn't have been much further wrong. **Surfing** is a **classic** – a book written when the Internet wasn't a tool talked about much but one that big companies used to sell stuff over. Instead it was a travelogue-type tale of J.C. Herz's adventures in the interactive world of Internet Relay Chat (IRC) and MUDs, in the pioneering days of the information superhighway. Since then, she has gone on to write **Joystick Nation**, a history of the video game.

talking to the nethead!

Your Roving Reporter brushed up on his keyboard reflexes and Quake cheat codes and went off to interview J.C. Herz:

Your Roving Reporter: Have you always been into computers, or have you got more nerdy with age? :-)

J.C. Herz: There was always a computer of one sort or another around the house while I was growing up – primitive video game terminals, and then the original IBM PC (what a dinosaur that was), and so on, but I was never seriously into them. Learned BASIC on an Apple II. Figured out DOS (but only so I could play Castle Wolfenstein with my brother). But I never got into coding, per se. Just word processing and the usual utilitarian stuff. The computer never became compelling to me until it became a communications device.

YRR: The Net . . . what's in it for you?

JCH: Email was, is, and always will be the killer app. The Web's all right for research, but that's definitely work-related, as opposed to something I'd do for fun.

YRR: You use MUDs quite a bit, right? Why do you like them so much?

JCH: MUDs were important when I was researching *Surfing*, because they're a very primitive version of some of the more sophisticated things that are evolving now – social spaces, communities, themed virtual environments, blah, blah. And I knew that it was important to understand them because they had the potential to evolve that way. They're petri dish experiments, growing (as all true innovations in cyberspace do) from the bottom up – fed by users. That said, I don't tend to spend that much time in them now, personally. Because if I'm going to invest that much time and energy in a fictional world, I'll write a damn novel.

YRR: How much coffee do you drink a day to survive long night 'marathons' researching (and playing) on-line? :–)

JCH: I don't even want to think about it. But then, it's all academic when you dispense with cups and go directly to intravenous drip!

YRR: Have you ever met anyone on-line that you just HAD to meet in RL?

JCH: No.

YRR: What's the 'trick' of using a MUD – any expert advice?

JCH: MUDs are a combination of architecture and play-acting. Write well and don't be a jerk.

YRR: So why do you think people like computer games so much?

JCH: Computer games do wonderful chemical things to your bloodstream. You face a fight or flight scenario, your body makes adrenalin. It's a kick. And then there are the more civilised puzzle-solving affairs which give you something beautiful to look at and put you in a state of deep, groovy concentration – flow. Either way, it's about escape. Immersion.

YRR: If you were creating a computer game, what would you include?

JCH: I'd want to play with time. You don't have to obey the laws of physics in a computer game, so why not?

YRR: What changes is the Net going to bring to gaming?

JCH: More people playing at once, apparently . . .

JC is also the first full-time digital entertainment critic of the New York Times. You can find her articles at the **http://www.nytimes.com**

MUDS

Here are the Web addresses of some popular MUDs. While MUDs are actually played over another part of the Internet called Telnet, the websites offer a lot of helpful info that you might like to read before connecting. If the MUD doesn't have a website, then of course I've just put in the Telnet address (remember you will need a Telnet program of some kind to use these).

Ancient Anguish **http://anguish.org**
Angalon – A Medieval Mud **http://angalon.tamu.edu/**
Asylum Mud **http://www.asylum-mud.org/**
Stick in the Mud – A Social Mud **telnet://mud.stick.org 9000/**
Toril: The Journey Continues **telnet://www.torilmud.com**

Other sites:

Mud List **http://mudlist.kharduin.net/**
As its main page says, 'If it's sites you're looking for, look no further'. This is the best collection of MUD links I could find on the Net – apart from Yahoo! of course . . .

QUAKE: WHEN THE GROUND SHAKES . . .

Run, Jump, Kill, Shoot, Maim and Destroy. These are just some of the scenes you encounter in Quake, a horrifyingly real game that is tremendously popular. 'Why?' some ask. Your Roving Reporter found 2 people who should know. Ehsan and Steve are **Quake** players who call themselves 'The Awesome Duo':

Your Roving Reporter: So, let's get straight to it. What is the fun in killing things?

Ehsan Gelsi: Well, there's a very distinct line between animated violence and actually stepping out in your local shopping mall and ripping people in half.

Steve Harland: It's just a great break from reality. It's tough to jump around the door of the bedroom and frag 4 enemies.

YRR: So what exactly is a 'frag'?

SH: A 'frag' is a kill. Every time a man falls, or explodes, you score a frag; top of the frag list at the end of the day wins.

YRR: J.C. Herz told me that on-line gaming means just being able to play with more people. But what is actually so fun about it? I mean, why kill with others, when you can kill by yourself?

SH: Well, it's much more fun if you can take on people around the world.

EG: A real-life opponent offers a greater challenge than running after a computer-controlled character with the same limited techniques. Computers can't think – humans can.

YRR: So do you kill them, too?

EG: Well, you can either team up or you can fight each other. But yeah, 'killing' is more fun.

YRR: I think we'll leave that there before the censorship man starts knocking at my door!

And it was lucky I did. After our recorded conversation, Steve and Ehsan showed me the stack of grenades they collect for fun, their army tank sitting out the back, as well as the rocket launcher hidden behind a flower pot! Well, not really . . .

It may come as a surprise, but thankfully, fighting games like *Quake* aren't the only ones available for play over the Internet. In fact, some of the best are the strategy-type games where you get to play God (and no, I don't have an interview with him/her).

So how do you find other people to play with? Well, in *Quake's* case you connect with a Clan. These are groups which meet on a regular basis to clash on-line. You can find the most up-to-date listing of these at Yahoo! by doing a simple search on *Quake*.

Toril — the Journey Continues

On-line gaming sites:

addresses

Wireplay **http://www.wireplay.com**
Available in Australia and the UK.

Total Entertainment Network (TEN) **http://www.ten.net**
Available in the USA.

And of course, where a specific service is unavailable, remember Kali (see page 128) is always available.

building

chapter eight

your home!

your Web page

there's no place like home

So you have been on the Net for a while and you've had a good look around the World Wide Web. You're an expert at email – and know how to act on USENET. You are well on the way to becoming a true cyber-citizen! All you need now is a Web page . . .

Luckily for you, this is remarkably easy, and anyone who can type can now produce HTML documents – the language of the Web. But by using the next few pages as a guide, you won't be producing just any old Web page. Hopefully by the end you'll have a snazzy, exciting and nicely designed website.

step-by-step guide

STEP 1. To put something on the Internet, you actually need 'a place to put it'. Fortunately you probably already have somewhere – your Internet Service Provider. Most ISPs provide customers with 1 to 25mb of Internet space for their websites. Check with your ISP about this before you start, because there are other options available (see below).

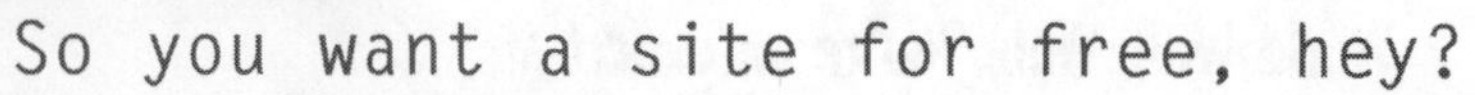
So you want a site for free, hey?

There are many places on the Web which are happy to provide you with some space to put your homepage on. Here are some of them:

- **Geocities –** The largest of the free homepage providers, Geocities has hundreds of thousands of users. Just go to **http://www.geocities.com**
- **Tripod –** Similar in style to Geocities. **http://www.tripod.com**

STEP 2. HTML authoring has come a long way from the early days when you had to type everything with a simple text editor in HTML coding. Now a huge selection of programs and

wizards are available to help you. In fact, in many instances you don't even need to see any HTML.

One thing that can do this, and is already owned by most people, is a word processor. Most word processor programs today (such as Microsoft Word) have special features that can directly turn their documents into HTML files. You just create the file using any of the usual features such as text, pictures, and tables and then save it as HTML. These word processors are particularly easy to use because the commands and buttons are very similar to the ones you usually use.

Once you've used these and think you have got the hang of it, you might like to use a professional Web design program such as Microsoft Frontpage, Macromedia Dreamweaver or Claris Homepage.

addresses

Microsoft **http://www.microsoft.com**
Macromedia **http://www.macromedia.com**
Claris **http://www.claris.com**

GOOD DESIGN

15-year-old Aleks Rzadkowski is known as The Saint on Internet Relay Chat, which Your Roving Reporter thinks is well justified.

The Sydneysider is the creator of heavenly websites that look so good I drool at the thought of having one similar (dream on, Nick). Last year Aleks's personal website (the one you can see above) was awarded an Honorable mention in the Australian Internet Awards.

addresses

http://www.softnexus.com.au/aleks/

STEP 3. So what are you going to put on your homepage? Well, that's a very good question!

It's always better to think about this before you start, or you will end up with a jumble of pages that have nothing to do with each other, all screaming out, 'This is a mess.' Remember that the idea is not just putting up an Internet page for the sake of it, so you need to add plenty of **content**. Try and write some original stuff and not just provide links to other places for information.

Some ideas for things to put on your homepage:

- information on your hobbies and interests. (What are you an expert on?)
- pictures and information about a celebrity or someone you like.

cute geek guy gal

- a joke page.
- an on-line art gallery, where you could scan some picture you made.
- a club.
- a service you could offer.
- a funny satire or parody of another site on the Web – although as you've probably realised these are already done to death and it might be hard coming up with something original to parody.

Hey Ladies! Look at me! I'm a dick!
THE DICK LIST

STEP 4. Adding **Style**. People don't like reading things from computer screens, and it is very hard to catch their attention with a simple page of text.

On the Web, things have to be exciting. So put in pictures and maybe even a few moving bits and pieces to add to the design. You'll need some graphics software to create these images. There are lots of different options around in the software area. Most pictures on the Internet are in the GIF or JPEG format, but even if you don't consider yourself an artist, many of these programs now virtually do the job for you – and it comes out looking very professional. The 'standard tool' is Adobe Photoshop, but this costs a lot of money, and there are cheaper ones such as Paint Shop Pro.

addresses

Adobe **http://www.adobe.com**
Paint Shop Pro **http://www.jasc.com**

STEP 5. An often overlooked problem with creating Web pages is getting people to notice them. The WWW is one heavily crowded place, and honestly, people will have absolutely no idea your homepage is even there. The best thing you can do to start is list your site in the many Search Engines and directories on the Internet.

A good place to start is a site called Submit-It at http://www.submit-it.com. Here you can send your entry to just about everywhere in one go. After that, try sending your site to a few awards or 'picks of the day'. If you can get chosen for one of these, you'll be on the way to plenty of visitors over time. Be patient and they will come. You might also like to send a note to a few related newsgroups about your new website.

HTML

I've explained how the World Wide Web allows you to display pictures and makes it easy to move from one document to another. Now this is only possible if there is a standard way of formatting (formatting is a computer word for 'how things look') for the various types of computers used to access the WWW. HTML is this standard. If you didn't have HTML you wouldn't have nicely designed pages with integrated graphics or be able to just click 'go' on a link to get to another page. HTML works with your browser and tells the browser how each bit of text should appear on the screen. Without the browser, HTML is just a plain text document, whatever it is called. For windows users, all this means is that the .txt extension has been changed to an .htm. Imagine you get out your text editor and start typing. Part of your HTML document might look like this in your text editor:

```
<B> Hello Welcome to my Web page </B><P>
```

Now, your document has been put onto the Internet. You open it with Netscape. Netscape is designed to recognise HTML files and it starts decoding the HTML into something slightly more readable by interpreting the meaning of the HTML tags.

The HTML tags are the parts in the < and >. When it gets to the part of the document above it will first pick out the text 'Hello Welcome to my Web page' and decide that it is intended to be displayed in the final presentation because it doesn't have any commands or triangular brackets around it. It will also note that it should be bold <B> and </B> and that there should be a paragraph break after the words <P>.

The HTML tags are being added to all the time to allow more options for website designers, and also include forms of multimedia and new technology.

How Stuff Works: Web Pages **http://www.howstuffworks.com/web-page.htm**

Web design etiquette

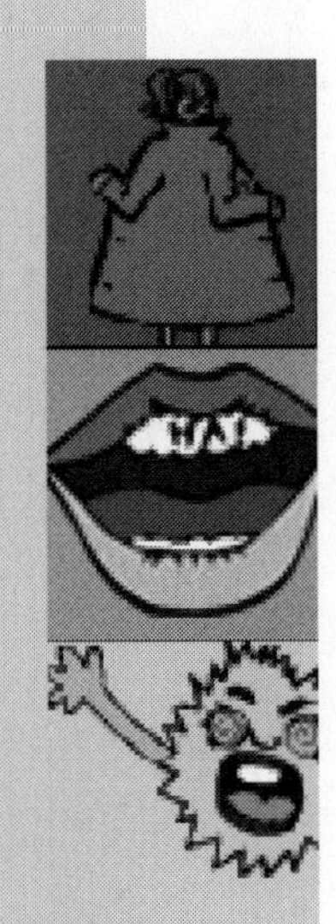

As well as the Netiquette I mentioned before, a new code has appeared in the last few months, and it is all about how to design appealing Web pages. Here are 10 of the worst things people can possibly do when creating Web pages:

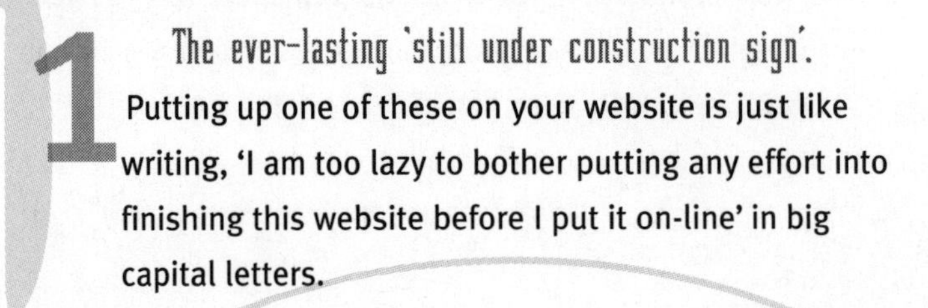

1 The ever-lasting 'still under construction sign'. Putting up one of these on your website is just like writing, 'I am too lazy to bother putting any effort into finishing this website before I put it on-line' in big capital letters.

2 Special Effects Overload. HTML and add-ons can now offer just about anything including blinking, moving, scrolling and ticking. One of these used in moderation may be fine, but don't use too many or you will make your visitors sick.

Vincent Flanders' Web Pages That Suck **http://www.webpagesthatsuck.com/home.html**

3. **The list of links of list of links of list of links phenomenon.** I'm sure your creative mind can come up with something a bit more interesting than links to other pages.

4. **'Error: 404 not found'.** If this comes up, it means that either a file is missing or a link is pointing to a faulty address. This is probably the worst thing that can happen to irritate your visitors. **DO NOT LET IT HAPPEN.** Make sure that links actually go some place.

5. **Frames.** Frames are one of the many tricks you can use to divide your homepage up into sections. If you are going to use them, try not to have more than a couple. Even though you think it may look good on your computer, the size of people's screens are often very different – and your nicely designed page may turn out a huge mess. Also, while tables are one of the best HTML tags (columns are much better than text that runs straight across the page), like frames, use them, but use them sparingly.

Pages That Suck

Learn Good Design by Looking at Bad Design

6 More is not necessarily better. The Internet is the perfect tool for publishing short notices and articles that change often. Posting 50,000 word documents doesn't work quite so well. Pictures and graphics are easy to read. Pages and pages of text in one big blob on screen are not. If you really have to put long documents on-line, why not break them up into lots of little sections and put links in between to give the visitors a rest.

7 Minimise the pictures. Most people have slow connections. They don't like having to wait a couple of minutes just to download some website. And if you are going to go heavy on the graphics, it better look good when it does load, or they certainly won't be back.

8 Stop the music. Just because you *can* have music, doesn't mean you *should*. Not everyone has everyone else's tastes, and if judged by the amount of mail you will receive you'd better remember it! Although if you have a theme website you could perhaps enhance it with music or sound effects.

9 Get your spelling right! Like email, the Web is not a place where you can start being slack about your spelling or grammar. As I've said before, it's best to check it, then check it again!

<u>Hometown AOL</u> **http://hometown.aol.com**

build better pages

10 One of the biggest mistakes that people make on the Internet is thinking that the citizens of the Net are interested in their every move, of every minute since they were born. Actually, no one could care less what you did on the 22nd of June 1998! And they are also not interested in your entire photo album. Probably, you can't do anything right with autobiographies on the Internet. The worst thing you can do is put a note in saying that your carefully crafted and detailed essay on your life is 'really boring, and you will find out more than you need to know' when obviously you don't think anything of the sort – or you wouldn't have wasted your time writing it!

BUILDING WEBSITES FOR $$$

Okay, okay – you are getting the hang of this Net thing, and now you're making websites . . . Well, let's just move one step ahead of all that – how about going professional? The media hype surrounding the Net has made every business in the land drool at the thought of owning their very own website. You and I know that website making is easy (although a good head for colours, and some expensive software is needed for the best results). However, the people who want the websites haven't caught on to that quite yet . . . So that means a lot of people wanting websites – and not enough people to make them. In business terms that means one thing. Big $$$$$.

Your Roving Reporter felt like he needed to cash in on this, but felt a bit guilty at the thought – and just decided to write a book! Anyway, one person he met along his travels was Steve Pate, the founder and manager of yet another enterprise (Oh no, you cry!) called Whaam!. Whaam! creates pretty slick-looking websites for many companies – for a fee. So here's what he said:

Your Roving Reporter: How did you get interested in the Net? Is your family computer mad?

Steve Pate: Ha, my family knows nothing about computers. We first got connected to the Internet as a present for my sister's birthday. After a while I ended up using the Net more than my sister and eventually stopped browsing the Net and started building websites.

YRR: So what made you create your different websites?

SP: Well, after a while I just started to realise that it would be actually quite possible for me to create my own websites so I started from scratch with a homepage at Geocities (most people start there). After a while I realised that I could do more and more so I purchased my own domain names and actually paid to have a proper, quality Internet account with 50 mb of Web space.

YRR: Do you do all the work or what?

SP: Yep. I do it all myself. From concept to completion. I particularly love the design side of things. The only time when I've actually hired someone to help me was when I needed some PERL programming done for a search engine which I created dedicated to adventure related websites.

YRR: I've found that being a teenager and being taken seriously is HARD (especially when you're trying to get a book published :-)). What are your thoughts on this? You seem to have some large contracts . . .

SP: Yes, it is extremely hard. I actually don't tell many of my clients how old I am. If they asked me I would tell them, but they don't ask so I figure that there is no point in causing a stir. If the people I deal with knew how old I was they would have an instant distrust for me which doesn't seem fair really.

YRR: What do you suggest for the readers who might be interested in website design or other Net projects?

SP: Okay. The best idea is just to muck around and experiment for a while first, and the best way to do this is to use a free homepage program like Geocities or something similar (there are a lot of them these days). If you think you've got the potential to go further then it's worth having a look around at some hosting services and actually paying for an account (if you can afford it). Building websites can be lots of fun and is very rewarding.

YRR: What is next for Steve Pate?

SP: By the time this is printed I will probably have created a million different websites as my ideas are always changing and some of my ideas are more successful than others. I guess I'll just keep trying new concepts until I find one that is very popular. I'm not sure if I'll pursue a career in the Internet industry, as acting is my main passion. For me this is just a bit of a hobby, a GREAT hobby.

Join GeoCities

addresses

Geocities **http://www.geocities.com**

and now for some advice from Gerald Tan . . .

Gerald Tan is the young creator of TeenWorld International, an enormous Malaysian-based group which runs a very successful website. He's also the winner of a number of Web design competitions, putting him up with the best. And he's got some advice just for you:

Your Roving Reporter: What process do you go through when creating a website – tools, time, thoughts . . . ?

● ● ● ● ● ● **GT:** At first, I'll need to really understand what the website is for, and what kind of website it is. Is it just going to be an on-line version of a brochure or is it going to be the kind of interactive and dynamic website that really harnesses the full power of the Internet? After that, I will develop a theme for the website, and in most cases, this has to suit the brand name of the company's corporate identity. I call this the 'feel' of the website. I will then take a look at the information I need to put on-line and group them into sections. I try to be very very organised when it comes to designing a structure of a website. Then, the actual development process starts – HTMLising, scanning, designing and layout. And then, of course, I will need to go through the website with the client and see what can be improved. You need lots of persistence and time. Appropriate tools really make a difference. I can't live without Adobe Photoshop. I always love to surf at nicely designed sites. It challenges me to do something better. I try to incorporate the ideas of those websites into my projects. You can call it learning by example. And one important thing: sometimes, it's better to get back to simplicity. As a Web designer, our job is not to amaze people with our skills. Our job is to get the message through in a fashionable, but most importantly, easily digestible way. If your bells and whistles distract visitors from getting your message, you have failed as a Web designer.

Related website:
TeenWorld International http://www.teenworld.com.my

Netaholics anonymous

Nerds, Junkies, Geeks – whatever you call them, they proliferate on the Web (where else?). Your Roving Reporter combed the Net, consulted the medical experts, and now publishes the symptoms . . . But don't worry – through early diagnosis, there could be a cure in sight . . .

the danger signs

Stereotypes abound when it comes to geeks (as I mentioned earlier in my introduction), and if possible it's best to try and stick to the scientific facts gleaned off the very reputable websites of some leading authorities in the field. I picked the top 10:

1. You find yourself brainstorming for new subjects to search.
2. You know your best friend's email address better than their name.
3. Your phone bill costs more than one third of your house.
4. You can name all the sites dealing with Australopithecus in alphabetical order in one minute.
5. Your dog has its own homepage.
6. You check your email. It says 'no new messages'. So you check it again.

7. **The last person you picked up was only a jpeg.**
8. **You name your children Eudora, Mozilla and Dotcom.**
9. **You hire a housekeeper for your homepage.**
10. **You start tilting your head sideways to smile.**

If you didn't smile to yourself throughout, then it's very likely you're not quite a nerd yet. However, if you thought 'Hey that's me' after every single one, then it's quite likely you're in need of some desperate therapy . . . consult your doctor now . . .

and

chapter nine
finally . . .

see you . . .

CU

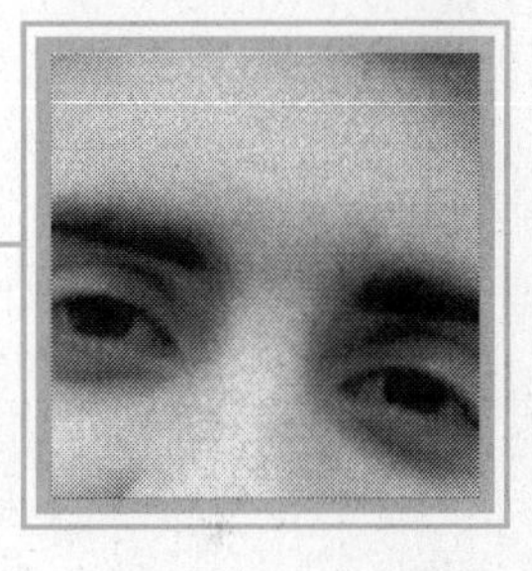

Well, I know I said very loudly not to put a whole lot of stuff about yourself on your webpage, but that doesn't have to apply to books! This last little bit is basically a short autobiography from a Netizen, and a few last words on the Net before I go.

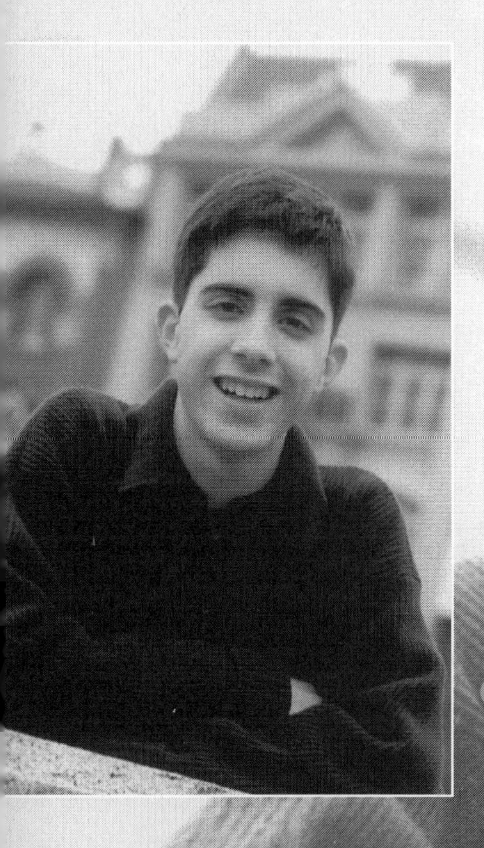

I jumped on the Net bandwagon (pretty much what you're doing) in the middle of 1995. The Internet was the bold frontier. As I said, I knew absolutely nothing about it then. **'What was it!', 'How do I use it!', 'Let's get home quickly so I can plug my modem in!'** were the kind of things going round in my head when we drove back across town after visiting a strange new place – a 'modem shop'.

Well, I plugged in, set myself up, dialled the service provider and . . . err . . . nothing happened. From memory I spent the next day fiddling around with the inside of my computer, the software and the modem – and thinking, **'Is this all some kind of scam?'** Surely not . . . With so many people involved, they couldn't possibly all keep the secret. Could they? Maybe they could? I was starting to have serious doubts. Anyway, I finally got it to dial. Then it started pouring out some terrible noises. I moved to the back of the room in case the modem was about to blow. 'No', said the ISP help desk (when I finally got through). That was usual – just some 'handshaking' thing or something. To me, handshaking meant something you do when you meet someone – and the noise didn't sound too polite!

But I was on the Net, hooorrraaaayyy – although, where to now? I suppose I finally got the hang of it and I'm sure you will as well. It's quite simple really. Just click and type.

Click.

I've met so many interesting and amazing people on-line that they are too numerous to mention (you will already have heard of many while reading through this book). But just quickly – there is Daniel, Kel and Lauren who spend huge amounts of time on their WKN activities, Martin who very much dislikes Bill Clinton (and almost everything else), the TCN chat room diva Nikki – as well as Tom, Mark, Chris, Kristel, Todd, and Gerald who have done a huge amount getting my club TCN going, and also Paul who just yells at everyone else. :-)

Getting 20 or 30 emails a day from right around the world, and trying to reply in some detail to at least most of them is a challenge, but it's something I've learned to accept. Almost.

So what am I saying here? That in the last 2 years I've had a 'life' on the Net? Certainly I have! Perhaps it's not been quite as fulfilling as that in RL, but it's been just as exciting.

AND A LAST WORD FROM ME . . .

The book is coming to an end. So far you've heard about part of what the Internet can do, and learnt how to deal with people, places and events on-line.

Hopefully you've also seen it in action, met some interesting people and had more than one encounter with the paranormal (that's normal). If so, you've probably spent a couple of days dabbling in HTML code and chatted away until late into the night. If not, jump into it now.

Goodbye new Net surfers. I hope I have prepared you for your adventures on-line. I hope you learn to like the Internet (how can anyone not?) and forgive it for its slowness and not go mad with impatience. ¶

happy
surfing
everyone –
there's a
big wave
coming!

:-)

books, books, books!

books

more words for your eyes

While I've tried to include a lot in my book – I admit, I've left things out (for the sake of interest and fun of course!). The following books will add to your knowledge. I can recommend them all. And all of these books can be bought on-line from websites such as Amazon (**http://www.amazon.com**) which claims to have over 2.5 million books.

Net Chick : A Smart-Girl Guide to the Wired World
by Carla Sinclair
Published by Henry Holt

Netstudy : Your Guide to Getting Better Grades Using the Internet and Online Services
Michael Wolff (Editor)
Published by Wolff New Media

The Truth is in Here : Conspiracies, Mysteries Superstitions, Kooks, and Cults on the Internet
by Karl Mamer
Published by Motion Works Pub

books

Creating Killer Web Sites : The Art of Third-Generation Site Design
by David Siegel
Published by Hayden Books

Surfing on the Internet: A Netheads Guide
by J.C. Herz
Published by Abacus

Joystick Nation : Your Complete Guide to Games on the Internet and Online Services
by J.C. Herz
Published by Abacus

name: Nick Moraitis
date of birth: 25/11/1982
address: Melbourne, Victoria, Australia
email address: nick@cyberjunkie.com
http://www.tcn.ml.org

Nick Moraitis is a 16-year-old, Year 11 student who alternates his time between St Kilda in Melbourne, Australia and a little place in the country called Yapeen (which no one has ever heard of – it's near Castlemaine, about 120 km from Melbourne). Nick's been using computers – and writing with them, ever since he was 7 years old, when he first published a weekly 'local' newspaper that went on to have over 60 subscribers around the world. An early adventurer onto the Internet, Nick is an avid chatter and email correspondent. It was this interest that led Nick to found the Teenage Computer Network in 1995 – now the Internet's leading user organisation for 12 to 20-year-olds interested in computers and multimedia, with over 6000 members. TCN operates on a non-profit basis, and offers an environment where communication between like-minded people can occur.

Nick's writing has appeared in Australian Personal Computer magazine and the Stand. He was also an on-again-off-again contributor to the Syte multimedia section in the Australian newspaper. Nick now contributes writing to Internet.au.

As well as his Internet adventures, Nick attends Girton Grammar School in Bendigo, Australia. Nick is a continually busy person and within school is a member of the Debating, Public Speaking, Choir, Internet and Magazine clubs. Nick learns Japanese, and he also studied piano and violin for a number of years.

A judge of the LOUD Australian National Youth Website Design Competition during January 1998, Nick thinks the on-line world offers younger people many great new opportunities to voice their opinions, communicate, and collaborate in a world-wide arena.

acknowledgements

PRELIMS: vi, cartoon of Bill Gates, Stale, http://www.stale.com; vi, CyberScience logo, CSIRO, http://www.csiro.au/; vii, Tamagotchi, Tamagotchi, http://www.bandaico.jp; vii, viii, flying girl, GIRL, http://www.worldkids.net/girl/; viii, cat playing card, The Bob Lancaster Gallery of Unusual Playing Cards, http://members.aol.com/rslancastr/blgupc/blgupc.htm; viii, house, CSIRO, http://www.csiro.au/; ix,

CHAPTER 0, INTRODUCTION: x, xiv, 1, xv, Queen Elizabeth & King Edward, Tudor England, http://tudor.simplenet.com.

CHAPTER 1, HOOKING UP TO THE NET AND HOW IT ALL WORKS: 2, 23, boy in chains, Cute Geek Guy Gallery, http://www.grrl.com/cuteboy.html; 5, dragon, Avalon, http://www.avalon-rpg.com; 5, world, NASA, http://www.nasa.gov; 6, James Bond, Geek Heroes, http://www4.ncsu.edu/unity/users/a/apdunsto/www/geek/geekheromain.html; 7, console of the BRLESC-I computer, U.S. Army Photo from K. Kempf, *Historical Monograph: Electronic Computers Within the Ordnance Corps*, http://ftp.arl.mil/ftp/historic-computers/; 17, tech-support cartoon, Joke Wallpaper.com, http://www.jokewallpaper.com; 18, 19, old phone & Big Pond logo, Telstra, http://www.telstra.com.au; 19, speed car and driver, The Aussie Invader Land Speed Record Challenge, http://invader.vrace.com; 21, logo, Netscape, http://www.netscape.com; 21, Internet Explorer logo, Microsoft, http://www.microsoft.com; 22, cow & logo, TUCOWS, http://www.tucows.com.

CHAPTER 2, LIFE AFTER CONNECTION: 24, 39, The Adventures of Cybergrrl, Cybergrrl, http://comics.cybergrrl.com; 28, map, Penguin Books Cartographic; 29, UltimateMegaSuperExcellentSearcher, Joke Wallpaper.com, http://www.jokewallpaper.com; 30–1, screen shots, Altavista, http://www.altavista.digital.com; 31, surfers & logo, Surfing New Zealand, http://www.surf.co.nz; 32, Pick of the Week award, Yahoo!, http://www.yahoo.com; 32, The Original Cool Site of the Day award; 32, surf images & logo, The Wet Surfing Page, http://surf.to.twsp/; 33, 34, 35, logos, Yahoo!, http://www.yahoo.com; 35, logo, Yahooligans!, http://www.yahooligans.com; 37, logo & Cool Dog Site of the Day award, Dogmark, http://www.sl.rim.or.jp/~ifo/d/dogmark.html; 38, masthead, Amazon, http://www.amazon.com.

CHAPTER 3, VIRTUAL LEARNING: 41, 44, 45, cartoon boy & maps, International Education Forum Australia, http://www.iefaust.org.au; 44, email envelope, The Spot, http://www.thespot.com; 46, 47, Kenny Sahr & logo, School Sucks, http://www.schoolsucks.com; 48, quotation from *Time* magazine taken from website, http://cgi.pathfinder.com/time/magazine/1997/dom/971124/notebook_tech.the_great_ter.html; 49, Adam & logo, The Net Atheists, http://yi.com/home/PerdigueroEusebio/nmg.html; 50, logo, Chuck Farnham's Weird World, http://monkey.hooked.net; 51, This Site is Safe for Kids & logo, Net Nanny, http://www.netnanny.com; 51, logo, CYBERsitter, http://www.solidoak.com/cysitter.htm; 51, logo, Safe Kids Online, http://www.safekids.com; 52, logo, Peacefire, http://www.peacefire.org; 52, dog, Cyber Snoop, http://www.pearlsw.com; 53, logo, KinderGuard, http://www.intergo.com; 54, Parliament House drawing & DEETYA image, Australian Federal Government, http://www.fed.gov.au/; 55, Pop Science TV & CyberScience logo, CSIRO, http://www.csiro.au/; 55, logo, ABS, http://www.abs.gov.au/; 55, search logo, NASA, http://www.nasa.gov; 56,' Around the Museum' image, Natural History Museum, http://www.nhm.ac.uk/; 56, Mauri image, National Archives of New Zealand, http://www.archives.govt.nz/; 56, logo, Corbis, http://www.corbis.com; 58, Natasha Stott Despoja, courtesy of AUSPIC; 59, 60, Australian Coat of Arms & government chart, Australian Federal Government, http://www.fed.gov.au/.

CHAPTER 4, SPOTLIGHT ON ENTERTAINMENT: 63, 80, Recovery TV, ABC, http://www.abc.net.au/recovery/; 67, 68, cartoons of Bill Gates & man blowing his nose, Stale, http://www.stale.com; 68–9, 70, plans & Steve cam, Steve's Wearable Wireless Cam, http://wearcam.org; 73–5, various cast members & banners, The Spot, http://www.thespot.com; 76, Garden page & Tamagotchi, Tamagotchi, http://www.bandaico.jp; 76, dog and cat, Petz Central, http://www.petz.com/central/default.asp; 77, 78, ' Scanning for Beam Down Location' and 'Boldly Go' banner, United Federation of Kids (UFK), http://www.ufk.org; 78, Hercules and Xena logo, Simutronics Corporation, http://www.play.net/simunet_public/hx/hxhome.asp; 79, 'As seen on ABC TV', ABC, http://www.abc.net.au/; 79, Triple J logo, ABC, http://www.abc.net.au/triplej/; 81, 82, Roger Davidson & Vivian Rose, The Teen Movie Critic, http://www.dreamagic.com/roger/.

CHAPTER 5, THE TRUTH IS OUT THERE: 84–5, 91, 93, 103, sky with alien image, International Society for UFO Research, http://www.isur.com; 87, flying saucer, UFO Folklore, http://www.qtm.net/~geibdan/; 88, salt and pepper shakers, The Doghouse Collection, http://www.doghaus.com; 89, logo, The 24 Hour Church of Elvis, http://www.churchofelvis.com; 92, masthead, Conspire.com, http://www.conspire.com; 92, logo, Illuminati Online, http://www.io.com; 93, sheep, http://www.sirius.com/~paulus/welcome2.html; 94, Geek glasses, Geek Week, http://www.geekweek.com; 94, Challenger space shuttle launch, Chuck Farnham's Weird World, http://monkey.hooked.net; 95, Agent Mulder, Geek Heroes, http://www4.ncsu.edu/unity/users/a/apdunsto/www/geek/geekheromain.html; 95, logo, The B Files, http://members.aol.com/TheBFiles/bfiles.htm; 95, 'Access Denied' stamp, The X Fools, http://www.xfools.com; 98, 100–101, shadowy woman, courtesy of Ruth Grüner; 99, 100, Kurt button, BLeAcH bUmS – BaNnErs, http://members.aol.com/Kurtcobuv/banner.html; 99, Courtney Love, The Dollhouse, http://brookelyn.com/dollhouse/hole/index.html; 99, portrait of Kurt Cobain, Marcus' Homepage: Gallery of the Dead, http://hhitfs.hh.se/~hk96mani/KC.htm; 100, Tom Grant, The Kurt Cobain Murder Theories, http://www.nirvanaclub.com/grant01.htm; 102, Bill Gates, Microsoft, http://www.microsoft.com/corpinfo/images/archive/.

CHAPTER 6, BECOMING A NETIZEN: 104, 121, portrait of George Washington, Archiving Early America, http://www.earlyamerica.com/; 105, Charlie Chaplin, Ed Stephan's Homepage, http://www.ac.wwu.edu/~stephan/; 108, No New Mail dialogue box, Joke Wallpaper.com, http://www.jokewallpaper.com; 108, yawning koala, http://www.onthenet.com.au/~jbergh/koala1.htm; 111, Marilyn Monroe, Marilyn Monroe Picture Gallery,

ledgem

http://members.tripod.com/~Krd/; 113, flying girl with star & logo, GIRL, http://www.worldkids.net/girl/; 114, logo, GUYS, http://www.worldkids.net/clubs/guys/; 114, logo, Girl Tech, http://www.girltech.com; 116, 117, old phone posters, Telstra, http://www.telstra.com.au/archives/museum/images/; 118, logo, Yahoo! Chat, http://chat.yahoo.com; 118, 'Chat Here Grrls!' banner, Cybergrrl, http://www.cybergrrls.com/; 119, 120, world, The Tidal Abyss, http://www.cyberteens.com/abyss/gallery/myworld.html.

CHAPTER 7, LIFE'S ALL FUN AND GAMES: 122, 135, figure in spacesuit, CNET Gamecenter.com, http://www.gamecenter.com/Peeks/Cc2/; 123, knight, Avalon, http://www.avalon-rpg.com; 125, Lara Croft, Geek Heroes, http://www4.ncsu.edu/unity/users/a/apdunsto/www/geek/geekheromain.html; 126, 134, dragons, Melissa's Homepage, http://www.infosights.com/~dluecke/melissa/index.html; 127, space battle, CNET Gamecenter.com, http://www.gamecenter.com/Peeks/Starfleet/; 128, 132, female mage & logo, Ancient Anguish, http://anguish.org; 129, 130, 131, alien, cat & Beavis playing cards, The Bob Lancaster Gallery of Unusual Playing Cards, http://members.aol.com/rslancastr/blgupc/blgupc.htm; 132, dragon, Avalon, http://www.avalon-rpg.com; 133, logo, Order of the Way Clan, http://www.order-of-the-way.org; 134, logo, Toril, http://www.torilmud.com.

CHAPTER 8, BUILDING YOUR HOME!: 136, 155, people in windows, courtesy of Ruth Grüner; 137, drawing of house, courtesy of Kaitlin Weaver (age 4 years); 139, house, CSIRO, http://www.csiro.au/; 140, island hut, Vahine Private Island Resort, http://www.ila-chateau.com/vahine; 141, signposts, Aleks' World, http://www.softnexus.com.au/aleks/; 142, masthead, Cute Geek Guy Gallery, http://www.grrl.com/cuteboy.html; 143, *NrrdGrrl!* tshirt, NrrdGrrl!, http://www.nrrdgrrl.com; 143, 'The Dick List', Disgruntled Housewife, http://www.disgruntledhousewife.com; 144, The Too Cool Award; 144, This Site Doesn't Stink Award; 145, screen shot & logo, How Stuff Works, http://www.howstuffworks.com/web-page.htm; 146, flasher, mouth & sun, Gurl Magazine, http://www.gurl.com; 147, Website creators & logo, Vincent Flanders' Web Pages That Suck, http://www.webpagesthatsuck.com/home.html; 148, 149, 'see the best pages', 'build better pages', 'know the guidelines' & 'talk about it' buttons, Hometown AOL, http://hometown.aol.com; 149, A Yahoo! Cool Site award, Yahoo!, http://www.yahoo.com; 151, Whaam! logo, Cyberteens, http://www.cyberteens.com/ezine/issues/interview/pate.html; 151, logo, Geocities, http://www.geocities.com; 152, logo, TeenWorld International, http://www.teenworld.com.my; 153, nerdy guy, Nerds On-Site, http://www.nerds.on.ca/; 154, nerdy guys, The Nerds, http://www.the-nerds.com/.

CHAPTER 9, AND FINALLY . . .: 159, 160, 161, 167, Nick Moraitis, courtesy of the author.

index

Hh

Ii

Jj

Kk

Ll

Mm

Nn

GRADE A
PASTEURIZED HOMOGENIZED
VITAMIN D CHOCOLATE MILK
MISSING
404 - Not Found
The requested object does not exist on this server. The link you followed is either outdated, inaccurate, or the server has been instructed not to let you have it.
ONE QUART (946 mL)